Communications
in Computer and Information Science   71

Latifa Boursas   Mark Carlson   Hai Jin
Michelle Sibilla   Kes Wold (Eds.)

Systems and Virtualization Management

Standards and the Cloud

Third International DMTF
Academic Alliance Workshop, SVM 2009
Wuhan, China, September 22-23, 2009
Revised Selected Papers

 Springer

Volume Editors

Latifa Boursas
Leibniz-Rechenzentrum (LRZ)
Garching, Germany
E-mail: boursas@tum.de

Mark Carlson
Oracle
Broomfield, CO, USA
E-mail: mark.carlson@oracle.com

Hai Jin
School of Computer Science and Technology
Huazhong University of Science and Technology
Wuhan, China
E-mail: hjin@hust.edu.cn

Michelle Sibilla
IRIT, Université Paul Sabatier
Toulouse, France
E-mail: sibilla@irit.fr

Kes Wold
Distributed Management Task Force, Inc.
Portland, OR, USA
E-mail: kes@woldconsulting.com

Library of Congress Control Number: 2010936642

CR Subject Classification (1998): H.4, C.2, H.3, D.2, H.5, I.2

ISSN   1865-0929
ISBN-10   3-642-14943-X Springer Berlin Heidelberg New York
ISBN-13   978-3-642-14943-6 Springer Berlin Heidelberg New York

springer.com

© Springer-Verlag Berlin Heidelberg 2010
Printed in Germany

Typesetting: Camera-ready by author, data conversion by Scientific Publishing Services, Chennai, India
Printed on acid-free paper   06/3180

Preface

This volume contains the proceedings of the Third International DMTF Academic Alliance Workshop on Systems and Virtualization Management: Standards and the Cloud (SVM 2009) held in Wuhan, China, during September 22-23, 2009.

The SVM 2009 proceedings are intended for use by students of systems and virtualization management. The reader is presumed to have a basic knowledge of systems management technologies and standards at the level provided, for example, by the Common Information Model (CIM) standard for modeling management resources. The student of systems management will find here material that could be included in an advanced study program. These proceedings should furthermore allow students to acquire an appreciation of the breadth and variety of systems and virtualization management research.

The proceedings also illuminate related standards and research issues, answering questions such as: what are the implications of virtualization for distributed systems management, which advances in information models and protocols aid in managing virtualization, what new problems will we incur when managing virtualized systems and services, and how might management itself benefit from virtualization? Topics related to managing distributed systems, virtualization of distributed resources/services and work in management standardization are also highlighted.

There were 28 regular paper submissions. These went through an active review process, with each submission reviewed by at least three members of the Program Committee. We also sought external reviews from experts in certain areas. All these inputs were used by the Program Committee in selecting a final program with 12 regular papers.

We gratefully acknowledge the support of Huazhong University of Science and Technology(HUST), headed by Hai Jin, through the provision of facilities and other resources, and our sponsor, the Distributed Management Task Force (DMTF).

Many individuals were very generous with their time and expertise. We thank the Program Committee and the external reviewers for their efforts in the assessment and evaluation needed to put together the technical program. We thank Hai Jin for his support in planning the logistics and his advice on organizing the conference.

We would especially like to thank the volunteers from the Huazhong University Local Committee for their assistance in running the workshop. We thank the system developers for creating and supporting the invaluable EasyChair conference management system. Finally, we thank Springer for providing complimentary copies of the proceedings of SVM 2009.

April 2010

Latifa Boursas
Mark Carlson
Hai Jin
Michelle Sibilla
Kes Wold

Organization

The SVM 2009 workshop was organized by the DMTF Academic Alliance in cooperation with Huazhong University of Science and Technology (HUST) and took place in Wuhan, China.

Organizing Committee

Latifa Boursas	Munich University of Technology, Germany
Mark Carlson	Sun Microsystems, Inc., USA
Hai Jin	Huazhong University of Science and Technology, China
Michelle Sibilla	IRIT, Paul Sabatier University, France
Kes Wold	Wold Consulting

Program Committee

Nazim Agoulmine	University of Evry Val d'Essone, France
Latifa Boursas	Munich University of Technology, Germany
Mark Carlson	Sun Microsystems, Inc., USA
Vitalian A. Danciu	Ludwig Maximilians University, Germany
Heinz-Gerd Hegering	Leibniz Supercomputing Centre, Germany
Wolfgang Hommel	Leibniz Supercomputing Centre, Germany
Bo Huang	Intel Research China
Minglu Li	Shanghai Jiaotong University, China
Xiaofei Liao	Huazhong University of Science and Technology, China
Jorge E. López de Vergara	Autonomous University of Madrid, Spain
Yingwei Luo	Peking University, China
Andreas Maier	IBM, Germany
Wenbo Mao	EMC China Research Lab, China
Gregorio Martinez	University of Murcia (UMU), Spain
Jishnu Mukerji	Hewlett Packard, USA
Michelle Sibilla	Paul Sabatier University, France
Zhiying Wang	National University of Defense Technology, China
Carlos Westphall	UFSC, Brazil
Weiming Zheng	Tsinghua University, China

Local Committee

Xiaofei Liao	Huazhong University of Science and Technology
Yingshu Liu	Huazhong University of Science and Technology
Xia Xie	Huazhong University of Science and Technology
Feng Zhao	Huazhong University of Science and Technology

Table of Contents

Power Management Challenges in Virtualization Environments

Congfeng Jiang, Jian Wan, Xianghua Xu, Yunfa Li, and Xindong You

Grid and Service Computing Technology Lab,
School of Computer Science and Technology,
Hangzhou Dianzi University, Hangzhou, Zhejiang, 310037, China
cjiang@hdu.edu.cn

Abstract. Power is becoming a critical resource to large scale server systems and data centers. With active deployment of virtualization technology, power management raise more challenges and have negative impact on system performance due to : (1) the isolation between the guest Virtual Machines (VMs) and the Virtual Machines Manager (VMM), and (2)the independent operation between multiple VMs. In order to improve the conventional per-Operating System power management techniques and make it possible to control and globally coordinate the power management policies for virtualized resources among all VMs and the VMM, new features and sophisticated designs must be integrated into the VMM or Hypervisor. In this paper a review is presented on the power management challenges in virtualization environments and some proposed solutions are compared. This paper also presents some discussions on the research topics on power management in virtualization environments.

Keywords: power management; virtualization; power estimation; workload characterization.

1 Introduction

Power consumption is becoming an annoying problem to not only mobile, wireless, and battery-powered devices, but also large scale server systems [1, 2, 3]. Lower power consumption can significantly extend the usage time of battery-powered devices or reduce heat-related malfunctions and Total Cost of Ownership (TCO) for enterprise server systems and data centers. Higher power consumption results in more heat dissipation, cooling costs and makes servers more prone to failures. Consequently, power consumption has become the most important design consideration for high-density servers. In large Internet-scale server systems and data centers, power saving technique is particularly valuable when applied to servers with multiple power supplies, where a partial failure of the power supply subsystem can result in a loss of performance in order to meet a lower power constraint or power budget [4]. For a successful power management solution, it must include power and cooling mechanisms employed. Nowadays, various emerging industrial solutions address different aspects of the problem. And the main focus of solutions is moving from the per-component, individual computer system to the internet scale data centers [5].

L. Boursas et al. (Eds.): SVM 2009, CCIS 71, pp. 1–12, 2010.

Virtualization has become a rapidly growing management solution for power saving in modern computing systems, especially in data centers. Traditional approaches to power management are based on operating systems with full knowledge of and full control over the underlying hardware. However, the distributed nature of multi-layered virtual machine environments makes such approaches insufficient. Moreover, reducing power consumption of data center in the presence of virtualization faces challenges include power consumption estimation and characterization, power management coordination among multiple Virtual Machines (VMs), and heterogeneity in hardware capabilities, which make it impossible to apply traditional power management techniques, such as coarser-grained device sleep or dynamic voltage/frequency scaling(DVS/DFS), directly to the virtualization environment without modification.

Although virtual activities are limited within a virtual machine and seem that they have no influence on real power consumption, virtual activities can still affect real power consumptions when they are mapping to real activities operated on the physical hardware eventually. Therefore, it is nontrivial to implement power management mechanism into the Hypervisor or Virtual Machines Manager (VMM) because fine-grained power management among various VMs can reduce more power consumptions significantly and can address additional problem such as power-aware job scheduling ,live VM migration, and power virus elimination.

Most of current power management schemes are limited to OS with monolithic kernel and not applicable for virtualization environments and most of current virtualization solutions usually virtualize a set of standard hardware devices only, without any special capabilities or support for power management. Therefore, it is necessary to outline the challenges of power management in virtualization environment. In this paper, a review is presented on the problem and some state-of-the-art proposed solutions of power management for virtualization environments are discussed. The remainder of this paper is organized as follows: In section 2 we analyze some implications of power management in virtualization environments. Section 3 presents an overview of various power management challenges, including power consumption estimation, coordination among VMs, etc. We also provide a simple comparison of some representative power management schemes applied in virtualization environment like Magnet [6], VirtualPower [7] and ClientVisor [8]. Finally, we summarize this paper and make some remarks on the research topics of the power management problem for virtualization systems in Section 4.

2   Implication of Virtualization Environment

The virtualization idea was proposed in 1960s when it was first developed by IBM to provide elegant and transparent concurrent, interactive access to an expensive mainframe computer. In the context of virtual machine, each VM is a duplicated, fully protected and isolated instance of the physical machine, which gives users an illusion of accessing the full physical machine directly [9]. Such a virtualization layer is called Virtual Machine Monitor (VMM), traditionally on top of the hardware and below the operating system. Since virtual machine provides time-sharing and resource-sharing on the highly expensive hardware and makes it possible to execute, develop, and test applications concurrently, it was widely used to reduce the hardware acquisition cost and improving the productivity by working on it simultaneously. Although hardware is becoming cheaper and modern operating systems are evolving as multitask and multi-user, virtualization is in renaissance again to address computer system problems, such as security, performance, reliability[8,10], and emerging applications such as execution of a range of applications, originally targeted for different hardware and OSes, on a given machine. Currently, server virtualization is a mainstream technology and various worldwide enterprises and organizations have adopted it as basic IT infrastructure to provide many benefits such as server consolidation, application and service consolidation, service isolation and encapsulation, sandboxing, multiple execution environments and multiple simultaneous OSes, virtual hardware, machine simulation and emulation, debugging, software migration, testing/QA, etc[11]. Moreover, virtualization is ever-growingly deployed in data centers for secure computing platforms, cloud computing infrastructure, power and cost savings, and other goals.

According to corresponding architecture and implementation, virtualization technology can be categorized on the basis of their abstraction levels, i.e., instruction set level, hardware abstraction layer (HAL) level, operating system level, library level and application level virtual machines [11].However, in the scope of and just for the discussion in this paper, we limit the virtualization concept to the operating system level. Currently, there are different virtualization software and may have different implementations. They can be simply divided into three models:

(1) Hypervisor model. In this model VMM is a middle layer between the operation system and the hardware and it also owns all the hardware. VMM provides all the virtualization functionality and implementation, such as CPU virtualization, memory virtualization, and I/O device virtualization. Two examples of this model are VMware ESXi® and Microsoft Hyper-V®, which are commercial virtualization solutions.

(2) Host-based model. In this model VMM is in residence at host operating system while the host OS owns all the underlying hardware, including CPU, memory, and I/O device. The VMM only acts as a kernel module or application and performs some of the host OS functionality, e.g. I/O device driver, scheduler. One example of this model is VMware Workstation®.

(3) Hybrid model. In this model VMM is a lightweight layer and only provides basic virtualization functionality, e.g., CPU and memory virtualization, leaving I/O device to a privileged VM (In Xen it called domain0). All the accesses to the I/O device are coordinated by this privileged VM through inter-VM communication. Two examples of this model are Xen [12] and KVM [13]. Please note that with some emerging hardware-assisted I/O virtualization technology support, the I/O device can be directly owned by a normal VM.

In summary, the main characteristics of virtualization can be summarized as follows:

(1) Transparency. In virtualization environment, the physical machine is transparent to end users and applications and gives users an illusion of accessing the full physical machine directly. The provided virtualization environment enables the users to develop or run application without knowledge of the underlying hardware. It is very useful for server consolidation among heterogeneous environments with legacy hardware and applications.

(2) Isolation. Instruction inspecting and trapping in virtualization provide isolation of a component from the rest of the physical machine [12]. This feature enables the

same physical hardware to be shared among hundreds of processes or applications in a time-shared manner by consolidating or dividing computing resources to many operating environments using methodologies like hardware and software partitioning or aggregation, partial or complete machine simulation, emulation, time-sharing, and others. Consequently, different operating domains are isolated and a software crash caused by one user cannot affect the systems used by other users on the same computing resource although only one software component can be in control of the processor at a time.

In presence of the transparency and isolation in virtualization environments, the implication of traditional approaches to power management that the operating systems are with full knowledge of and full control over the underlying hardware, can not hold anymore. Since the VMM usually does not know what the VMs are doing and the VM are unaware of the activities of the underlying hardware, it is blind for the corresponding VMs to implement the power management decisions. Moreover, since the VMM are unaware of the activities of the high level applications, it is hard to make power management decisions without sufficient workload power characteristics. In the following, we will analyze the power management challenges facing to virtualization environments, including power consumption estimation and coordination among VMs.

3   Power Management Challenges in Virtualization Environment

Virtualization provides flexible construction of numerous virtual machines with almost no hardware limitations, and consequently reduces the total cost of ownership. It also enables to better exhaust available hardware resources. However, conventional approaches to control power consumption, for example, Dynamic Voltage/Frequency Scaling (DVS/DFS), may not be simply imported to virtualization environment without modifications, particularly for data centers with heterogeneous machines and legacy OSes. In this environment, various virtual machines usually require different power management operations. A global cooperative power management mechanism for VMM to coordinate between numerous VMs to agree on one single operating state is not available, and usually impossible. Therefore, moving the power consumption control mechanism from hardware-level to fine-grained software-level is indispensable and more promising for virtualization environments, and has the potential to reduce more power consumption with additional support of VMM and the physical machines. Some key challenges and constraints to achieve this goal are listed in the following.

3.1 Power Consumption Estimation of VMs

In order to implement fine grained power management for power consumption reduction in virtualization environment, the first step is to estimate the power consumption of the corresponding VMs. In non-virtualization environments, power consumption of the hardware can be directly divided to the applications using approaches such as code profiling and hardware performance counters based power consumption estimation. However, in virtualization environments the power consumption should be accounted to individual VM and the guest operating system can then split it between its applications, since VMM do not have knowledge of the upper level activities beyond it. The VMM can only obtain coarse-grained per-VM power consumption information but has no knowledge of the power consumption of individual applications inside every VM. This manner of dividing power consumption between VMM and VMs provides fine-grained power management feasibility and power-aware VM scheduling and migration.

Approaches to profile the power usage of applications play a main role for power management support in current non-virtualized systems [14, 15]. Power-driven statistical sampling and thread-level power estimation are main techniques to estimate power consumption. In practical implementation, power estimation techniques for power management should not add to additional overheads or impede prediction accuracy and runtime performance under various workloads. Lee and Brooks [16] proposed regression modeling as an efficient approach for accurately predicting performance and power for various applications executed on any microprocessor configuration in a large micro-architectural design space. Sinha et al [17] proposed a software energy estimation technique using instruction level profiling. ECOSystem [18] uses resource containers for power consumption estimation of mobile systems. This modified Linux kernel estimates the power consumption through different states of each device, e.g. standby, idle, and active, and measures the time a device spends in the respective state.

Since there are numerous devices and device drivers in virtualization environment, it is important to be able to adapt to new devices easily for power estimation with minimal changes to the driver that is managing the device. In order to divide the power consumption of physical devices accurately between the VMs, the VMM has to track each device activity to the originating VM and the VM will split it to virtual devices such as CPUs, memories, and hard disks. However, in virtualization environments, devices are usually shared among multiple VMs, i.e., there are interactions between different devices. Therefore, the estimated power consumption of physical devices must be mapped to the virtual devices by the VMM in a manner that enables effective guest-level power management. This requires a systematic and per-device power consumption model for both VMM and VMs.

The hardware performance counters and event logging [19] are often used for power estimation. The power consumption of each VM can be calculated using the tracing data of performance counters and log buffers. However, since the performance counter logs are relatively small and easy to fulfill, the sampling period should be regulated to a proper value. Moreover, prediction accuracy has impact on VM behavior and program execution time.

3.2 Power Management Coordination among VMs

Traditionally, only one software component can control the processor at a time and be able to execute a privileged instruction and the operating system kernel has full control of the hardware. Based on this feature, most current approaches to power management are developed only for standard, legacy OSes with a monolithic kernel which has full control over all hardware devices and their operating modes [20]. The monolithic kernel can regulate the device activities or power consumption directly to meet power constraints or budgets and it also controls the whole execution flow in the system. Therefore, it can easily track the power consumption at the application level to achieve dynamic and comprehensive power management.

But the condition changes in modern virtualization environments because there are distributed and multi-layered software stack including VMM, multiple VMs, device driver modules, and other service infrastructure [20]. Another trend in modern virtualization environment is that the VMM will perform a maximal set of device control in unprivileged driver domains [21, 22, 23] and VMM has direct control over a small set of devices. In contrast, the guest OSes, have full knowledge of their own applications but operate on non-privileged virtualized devices, without direct access to the physical hardware, and are unaware that the hardware may be shared with other VMs. In such an environment, direct and centralized power management is unfeasible, as device control and power consumption information are distributed across the whole system. At the bottom level of the virtualization environment, the privileged hypervisor and host driver modules have direct control over hardware devices and their power consumption. In such a scenario, the unprivileged power management operation by individual VMs should be trapped into the kernel and the kernel executes the instruction. Therefore system-wide power management among multiple VMs is usually hard to achieve because numerous VMs providing different services have different power management policies and cannot agree on a single operating condition or configuration. Furthermore, the whole situation is getting even worse because the guest OSes are also unaware of the side effects on power consumption caused by individual regulation.

Moreover, the pattern of various server virtualization deployment solutions has lead to the creation of multiple heterogeneous server virtualization environments within single data center or organization. And with heterogeneity comes power management problem and constraints, which have a negative impact on server virtualization and overall system performance, especially for heterogeneous server virtualization environments with multiple heterogeneous and legacy applications and hardware.

Consequently, quantifying the physical power consumption into individual VM and translating it from a global, system-wide into a local, per-VM one is the key challenge for power management within and across VMs in virtualization environment. A system-wide power consumption constraints among all guest OSes and driver or service components must be integrated into the VMM in order to coordinate the power consumption of physical devices and the allocation of physical devices to each VM. When various power management decisions are made by the corresponding guest OSes, a global coordination mechanism responsible for coordinating power management among VMs should be developed and triggered. System-wide power management ensures that the VMM performs in coarse-grained manner and independent of the guest operating system. Meanwhile, guest OS can benefit from fine-grained, application-level knowledge of power consumption because the guest OS can regulate the allocation of virtual devices to ensure that its applications under its given power constraint or budget.

3.3 Comparison of Existing Solutions

There are some elegant schemes proposed to reduce power consumption in virtualization environment.

Nathuji and Schwan [7] proposed a VirtualPower Management (VPM) framework which uses the combination of hard and soft scaling for virtualized enterprise systems. The framework consists of PM (Power Management) states, VPM channels, VPM rules and VPM mechanisms which try to address the challenges including coordination among VMs, multiple VMs per physical machine, and heterogeneity in hardware capabilities and power characteristics. They use synthetic transactional benchmarks and RUBiS application, with power measured directly at the outlet and they get 34% gain from consolidation onto Intel Core processor.

Previous local approaches focus on power reduction of the components in a single workstation without a global vision on the whole cluster and only applicable to homogeneous workstations and specific applications, Hu et al [6] proposed a novel approach, named Magnet, which uses live migration of virtual machines to transfer load among the nodes on a multilayer ring-based overlay. Their scheme can reduce the power consumption greatly by regarding all the cluster nodes as a whole and can be applied to both the homogeneous and heterogeneous servers. Their experimental measurements show that the new method can reduce the power consumption by 74.8% over base at most with certain adjustably acceptable overhead.

In contrast to power management in consolidated servers, it is very different to manage power in virtualized desktop environment, e.g., a virtualized desktop environment consists of a VMM and three asymmetry guest domains, i.e., a control domain, a background domain and a primary user domain [8]. Since the conventional OS can not directly access and control the hardware in virtualization environments, the existing power management solutions for server consolidation are usually VMM-centric, i.e., the VMM gathers the power management decisions of the guests as hints, and makes the final decision to manipulate the hardware, e.g., the power management in Xen 3.3 release. However, this scheme does not work well in desktop virtualization environment because there are frequent interactions between the OS and the users. To address this problem, Chen et al [8] proposed the ClientVisor scheme for power management of COTS (Commercial-Off-The-Shelf) operating system, which hosted in the primary user domain in the virtualized desktop environment where VMM coordinates the power management decisions of the guests only at the "key points". That is, the guest OS directly manages the power of processor and devices except the sensitive ones such as NIC and the VMM will coordinate the power management decisions made by the guest domains only at the "key points", e.g., when the primary user domain decides to put CPU in a sleep state. A power reduction of 22% is achieved in their prototype implementation and experiments in the static power usage scenario.

Traditional approaches to power management are based on operating systems with full knowledge of and full control over the underlying hardware. However, the distributed nature of multi-layered virtual machine environments renders such approaches insufficient. Stoess et al [20] presented a novel framework for power management in modular, multi-layered operating system structures, which provide a unified model to partition and distribute energy, and mechanisms for energy-aware resource accounting and allocation. And the framework explicitly takes the recursive power consumption into account, which is spent, e.g., in the virtualization layer or subsequent driver components.

Table 1 shows a simple comparison of the above three power management schemes in virtualization environments.

Table 1. Comparison of three power management schemes

Metrics\schemes	VirtualPower	Magnet	ClientVisor	Ref.[20]
Testbed configuration	Multiple PCs machines with Intel Dual Core Pentium 4 processors	A 64-hosts cluster with AMD Athlon 3500+processors	Desktop virtualization environment with Intel Core2 Duo T9400 processor	A machine with Intel Pentium D processor
Hardware Heterogeneity	Identical +Heterogeneous	Homogeneous	Homogeneous	Homogeneous
VMM	Xen	Xen	Xen	L4 micro-kernel
Using DVS/DFS	Yes	N/A	N/A	N/A
Number of VMs	>=4	N/A	3	N/A
Online/Offline	online	online	online	online
Power consumption estimation	measured 'at the wall'	N/A	measured 'at the wall'	external high performance data acquisition (DAQ) system
Power management coordination	(i)system-level abstractions including VPM states, channels, mechanisms, and rules (ii)VM-level 'soft' power scaling mapping to real power states and scaling	centric, concentric non-overlapping rings with heartbeats exchange	coordinate only "at the key points"	budget allotment
Max. Power savings	34%	74.8%	22%	N/A
Overheads	Little performance penalties	Adjustably acceptable	Degration about 2%~3%.	N/A
With QoS/SLA guarantees	Yes	Yes	N/A	N/A
VM migration	Yes	Yes	N/A	N/A
Workload	RUBiS	bit-r, m-sort, m-m, t-sim, metis, r-sphere, and r-wing	SPECpower_ssj	DAQ/bzip2 application

N/A: stands for not mentioned in the corresponding paper.

We observe from Table 1 that DVS/DFS schemes are not utilized in most of the existing solutions for power management in virtualization environments due to the complexity of multiple scaling modes coordination among various VMs. In contrast, they use VM migration for consolidation and to save more power consumptions since it is much easier to implement VM migration for the underlying VMM or hypervisor. However, this does not mean that VMs can randomly be migrated among all nodes. Actually, the potential overheads caused by live migrations of VMs can not be ignored in many cases because they may have severe negative impacts on global system performance including Quality of Service (QoS) and Service Level Agreements (SLAs) satisfactions.

Moreover, in large data centers with legacy hardware and software applications, it is impossible to implement global DVS/DFS schemes among all machines due to the heterogeneity. Therefore, more power reduction can be achieved if fine grained DVS/DFS schemes are used elegantly in virtualization environments.

4 Discussion

Power consumption has emerged as a critical issue in large scale computing systems. Server virtualization consolidates multiple under-utilized servers into a single physical server to exhaust physical machines. However, this advantage of virtualization also leads itself to the original power consumption problem because there usually are high power densities in virtualization environments. Due to the high-density of service consolidation and development of new applications and the increasing number of users with heterogeneous requests in virtualization environments, providing users with SLA guarantees while executing applications and saving power consumption has become a crucial challenge that needs to be addressed.

It is important to reduce power consumption in virtualization environments. This paper provides a review of current research on power management issues in virtualization environments. It can be summarized as follows:

(1) VM-level power management is necessary for fine-grained power control in computing systems with virtualization deployment. And it is feasible to save more power consumption from a software-level standpoint. However, due to the lack of comprehensive control over and knowledge of the power consumption in the virtualization system, there exist challenges for power management in virtualization environments. For example, conventional hardware based per-component and system-wide power management methods can not save considerable power consumptions because they are coarse-grained and not adaptive to various fluctuating workloads in real virtualization environments.

(2) Power estimation and accounting is the first concern for saving power consumption since multiple VMs may share the same device at the same time. And the first step for power management is to estimate the power consumption of the implemented physical devices. Consequently, conventional power estimation techniques do not work well in virtualization environments without modifications because they are designed only for monolithic kernels. In virtualization environments, the power consumption of the undertaken hardware can not be separated directly to the VMs and the upper applications due to the presence of the VMM and the transparency nature of virtualization. Therefore, elegant techniques, such as instruction-level and thread-level power profiling and accounting for splitting power consumptions between VM in VMM level and its applications in VM level are needed. Furthermore, the hardware performance counter recording and event logging will add on additional overheads on system performance.

(3) In order to coordinate power management among multiple VMs along with different workload characteristics and access modes, especially with simultaneous on-demand provisioning and accesses of shared physical infrastructures to VMs, regulation point of power consumption must be negotiated among these VMs. However, a global cooperative power management mechanism for VMM to coordinate between numerous VMs to agree on one single operating state is not available, and hard to achieve it. Moreover, simultaneous accesses of shared physical infrastructures make it harder for the VMM to fulfill the SLAs or QoS requirements with least cost among multiple VMs. And the system performance can be deteriorated greatly if the objective is to minimize the total power consumptions separately, despite of the violations of SLAs requirements of VMs.

(4) To reduce more power consumption or to balance the power consumption of processors, fine grained power management usually requires migration of applications, tasks or processes from and to different VMs. However, migration overheads must be considered in both sensor-based or performance counter-based migration techniques. For example, VM migrations among various hosts and protection domains cost much network traffic and long application downtime, especially for memory intensive workloads because the runtime memory state of the VM must be transferred and synchronized with the guidance of memory copy or trace data[24]. Another problem is how to characterize the power consumption patterns of processes to identify hot spots, i.e., hot tasks or hot VMs that cause high power consumptions. Power-aware job scheduling or VM scheduling and migration with external constraints such as SLAs or QoS may avoid this kind of power imbalance issue.

Although there are also tradeoffs such as latencies, performance degradations, conflicts and coordinations, between the power reduction and performance of the specific application, it's worthy of implementing a bin-level power management schemes to reduce power consumption as much as possible in virtualization. However, there are also dependencies and priorities between the given issues mentioned above. Power estimation is fundamental for power management because power consumption must be measured and estimated before any power management decisions are made. When implementing power management decisions, coordination and negotiations should be done to achieve global agreements on final power regulations. To achieve better power/performance balancing jointly and to avoid hot spots of power consumption, VM or task level migration may be issued among multiple hosts. Moreover, to minimize the total power consumptions while still maintaining the system performance in real scenarios, SLAs constraints must be considered.

With the ongoing trend of virtualization and emerging hardware, the power management problem is still active and researchers and engineers are still trying to address this issue through various efforts. It is highly likely that combination of VMM level and VM level power management can overcome this power management problem and provide better performance for virtualized systems.

Acknowledgments. The funding supports of this work by State Key Development Program of Basic Research of China (Grant No. 2007CB310900), Natural Science Fund of China (NSFC) (Grant No. 60873023), and Hangzhou Dianzi University Startup Fund (Grant No. KYS 055608058), are greatly appreciated.

References

1. Venkatachalam, V., Franz, M.: Power Reduction Techniques for Microprocessor Systems. ACM Computing Surveys 37, 195–237 (2005)
2. Jiang, C., Xu, X., Wan, J., You, X.: Energy Management for Microprocessor Systems: Challenges and Existing Solutions. In: The 2nd 2008 International Symposium on Intelligent Information Technology Application Workshop, pp. 1071–1076. IEEE Computer Society Press, Los Alamitos (2008)

3. Srikantaiah, S., Kansal, A., Zhao, F.: Energy Aware Consolidation for Cloud Computing. In: The 2008 USENIX Workshop on Power Aware Computing and Systems at OSDI 2008 (HotPower 2008). USENIX Association, Berkeley (2008), http://www.usenix.org/event/hotpower08/tech/full_papers/srik antaiah/srikantaiah_html/

4. Wang, X., Lefurgy, C., Ware, M.: Managing Peak System-level Power with Feedback Control. Technical Report, IBM Research (2005)

5. Ramos, L., Bianchini, R.: C-Oracle: Predictive Thermal Management for Data Centers. In: IEEE 14th International Symposium on High-Performance Computer Architecture (HPCA-14), pp. 111–122. IEEE Computer Society Press, Los Alamitos (2008)

6. Hu, L., Jin, H., Liao, X., Xiong, X., Liu, H.: Magnet: A Novel Scheduling Policy for Power Reduction in Cluster with Virtual Machines. In: The 2008 IEEE International Conference on Cluster Computing (Cluster 2008), pp. 13–22. IEEE Computer Society Press, Los Alamitos (2008)

7. Nathuji, R., Schwan, K.: Virtualpower: Coordinated Power Management in Virtualized Enterprise Systems. ACM SIGOPS Operating Systems Review 41, 265–278 (2007)

8. Chen, H., Jin, H., Shao, Z., Yu, K., Tian, K.: ClientVisor: Leverage COTS OS Functionalities for Power Management in Virtualized Desktop Environment. In: The 2009 ACM SIGPLAN/SIGOPS International Conference on Virtual Execution Environments (VEE 2009), pp. 131–140. ACM Press, New York (2009)

9. Smith, E.J., Nair, R.: The Architecture of Virtual Machines. Computer 38, 32–38 (2005)

10. Figueiredo, R., Dinda, A.P., Fortes, J.: Resource Virtualization Renaissance. Computer 38, 28–31 (2005)

11. Nanda, S., Chiueh, T.: A Survey on Virtualization Technologies. Technical Report, Department of Computer Science, SUNY at Stony Brook (2005)

12. Barham, P., Dragovic, B., Fraser, K., Hand, S., Harris, T., Ho, A., Neugebauer, R., Pratt, I., Warfield, A.: Xen and the Art of Virtualization. In: The 19th ACM Symposium on Operating Systems Principles (SOSP 2003), pp. 164–177. ACM Press, New York (2003)

13. KVM, http://www.linux-kvm.org/

14. Curtis-Maury, M., Dzierwa, J., Antonopoulos, C.D., Nikolopoulos, D.S.: Online Power-Performance Adaptation of Multithreaded Programs Using Hardware Event-Based Prediction. In: The 20th Annual International Conference on Supercomputing (ICS 2006), pp. 157–166. ACM Press, New York (2006)

15. Gurumurthi, S., Sivasubramaniam, A., Irwin, M.J., Vijaykrishnan, N., Kandemir, M., Li, T., John, L.K.: Using Complete Machine Simulation for Software Power Estimation: The SoftWatt Approach. In: The 8th International Symposium on High Performance Computer Architecture (HPCA-8), pp. 141–150. IEEE Computer Society Press, Los Alamitos (2002)

16. Lee, B.C., Brooks, D.M.: Accurate and Efficient Regression Modeling for Micro-Architectural Performance and Power Prediction. In: The 12th International Conference on Architectural Support for Programming Languages and Operating Systems (ASPLOS-XII), pp. 185–194. ACM Press, New York (2006)

17. Sinha, A., Ickes, N., Chandrakasan, A.P.: Instruction Level and Operating System Profiling for Energy Exposed Software. IEEE Transactions on VLSI 11, 1044–1057 (2003)

18. Zeng, H., Fan, X., Ellis, C., Lebeck, A., Vahdat, A.: ECOSystem: Managing Energy as a First Class Operating System Resource. In: The 10th International Conference on Architectural Support for Programming Languages and Operating Systems (ASPLOS-X), pp. 123–132. ACM Press, New York (2002)

19. Stoess, J., Uhlig, V.: Flexible, Low-overhead Event Logging to Support Resource Scheduling. In: the Twelfth International Conference on Parallel and Distributed Systems (ICPADS 2006), vol. 2, pp. 115–120. IEEE Computer Society Press, Los Alamitos (2006)
20. Stoess, J., Lang, C., Bellosa, F.: Energy Management for Hypervisor-Based Virtual Machines. In: The 2007 USENIX Annual Technical Conference (USENIX 2007), pp. 1–14. USENIX Association, Berkeley (2007)
21. Fraser, K., Hand, S., Neugebauer, R., Pratt, I., Warfield, A., Williamson, M.: Safe Hardware Access with the Xen Virtual Machine Monitor. In: The 1st Workshop on Operating System and Architectural Support for the On-Demand IT Infrastructure (the OASIS ASPLOS 2004 workshop) (2004),
    http://www.cl.cam.ac.uk/research/srg/netos/papers/2004-oasis-ngio.pdf
22. LeVasseur, J., Uhlig, V., Stoess, J., Götz, S.: Unmodified Device Driver Reuse and Improved System Dependability via Virtual Machines. In: The 6th Symposium on Operating Systems Design and Implementation (OSDI 2004), pp. 17–30. USENIX Association, Berkeley (2004)
23. Rosenblum, M., Garfinkel, T.: Virtual Machine Monitors: Current Technology and Future Trends. Computer 38, 39–47 (2005)
24. Liu, H., Jin, H., Liao, X., Hu, L., Yu, C.: Live migration of virtual machine based on full system trace and replay. In: The 18th ACM International Symposium on High Performance Distributed Computing (HPDC 2009), pp. 101–110. ACM Press, New York (2009)

Chinese Wall Isolation Mechanism and Its Implementation on VMM

Guanhai Wang, Minglu Li, and Chuliang Weng

Department of Computer Science and Engineering,
Shanghai Jiao Tong University, Shanghai 200240, China
`tierwang@sjtu.edu.cn`, `li-ml@cs.sjtu.edu.cn`

Abstract. Virtualization is achieving increasing popularity and there are some mandatory access control (MAC) mechanisms available which control overt communications among virtual machines (VM) in virtual machine systems. However such mechanisms cannot block covert channels. A strong isolation mechanism at hardware layer can benefit solutions to this problem. Hence, in this paper we propose an isolation mechanism based on Chinese Wall policy to make an air-gap among VMs which have conflict of interest, and implement it on a popular virtual machine monitor (VMM), Xen. It regulates the VMM allocating hardware resources like physical memory, CPUs and I/O adapters to VMs without many losses of system performance. Hence it provides stronger isolation among VMs than VMMs do.

1 Introduction

As the widespread use of virtualization technologies, more and more security issues of virtualization are raised. Paul A. Karger [1] suggested that although a very small and simple VMM may have less security vulnerabilities, virtualization itself cannot directly offer benefits to security of computer system. Then some MAC mechanisms, for example sHype/Xen [2], have appeared and are available on some VMMs now. But Trent Jaeger, Reiner Sailer and Yogesh Sreenivasan [3] showed that such MAC mechanisms may also contain covert channels and proposed an approach to manage possible covert leakage.

Although VMMs provide good isolation mechanisms to separate runtime environment of VMs. We believe that a stronger isolation mechanism than those provided by VMMs offers substantial help to solving this kind of security problems. So in this paper we propose a Chinese Wall Isolation (CWI) mechanism, which not only provides stronger isolation than VMMs do but also takes full advantages of virtualization technologies simultaneously. We choose classical Chinese Wall security policy [4] to model our mechanism, then implement it on the Xen VMM [5].

The rest of this paper is structured as follows. In Sect.2 we summarize some related work. Sect.3 states our design and Sect.4 states our implementation. Sect.5 evaluates CWI's overheads and impacts on security and hardware resources utilization. Finally the paper ends with some conclusions in Sect.6.

L. Boursas et al. (Eds.): SVM 2009, CCIS 71, pp. 13–18, 2010.

2   Related Work

As the development of virtualization technologies, on the one hand some researches like NetTop [6] focus on using virtual machines to create a more secure computer system. On the other hand many researches like sHype/Xen and PCW model [7] focus on building MAC mechanisms to improve security of virtual machine systems.

sHype/Xen is an MAC mechanism based on Type Enforcement policy and Chinese Wall policy. PCW model is also based on Chinese Wall policy while its policy is stricter than the Chinese Wall policy in sHype/Xen. Suppose that there are some VMs which compete against each other and VM1 is one of them. If VM1 is running, the others cannot run at the same time according to the Chinese Wall policy in sHype/Xen. While if VM1 and some VMs not competing against VM1 are running concurrently, the others competing against VM1 cannot run till VM1 and all its company are not running according to the Chinese Wall policy in PCW.

3   Mechanism Design

D. F.C. Brewer and M. J. Nash defined the key concepts of classical Chinese Wall model in [4] as follows. An analyst is defined as a subject. The files containing information are defined as objects. All objects about the same company are grouped into a company dataset. All company datasets whose companies are in competition are grouped together and one group is a conflict of interest class. The access rule is that when a subject requests access to an object, the access is granted if and only if the requested object a) is in a company dataset which the subject has accessed before, or b) belongs a conflict of interest class to which the subject hasn't access any objects belonging. We just adjust the definition of objects and subjects. VMs containing information about a company are defined as objects. And hardware resources, such as physical CPUs, physical memory pages, and I/O adapters, are defined as subjects. If one physical CPU has more than one cores, it is also defined as one subject. We define the time from a virtual machine system booting up to rebooting or power-down as a session.

The VMM must keep all subjects' previous access histories to enforce the access rule in one session. In our prototype the VMM uses one 32-bit record to keep one unit of hardware's previous access history. The 32-bit record is divided into eight groups of four binary digits. Each group of four binary digits represents a dataset ID and is written as a hexadecimal digit $d_i (i = 1 \cdots 8)$. Therefore a hexadecimal string "$d_1 d_2 d_3 d_4 d_5 d_6 d_7 d_8$" denotes a 32-bit record. A dataset ID $d_i (i = 1 \cdots 8)$ in a 32-bit record must belong to a unique conflict of interest class c_i, and therefore there is a maximum of eight conflict of interest classes in the prototype. Every conflict of interest class may have a maximum of 15 datasets since $d_i = 0$ means that the subject has not access any objects belonging to the conflict of interest class c_i.

Every dataset is assigned one label which comprises a dataset ID and a conflict of interest class ID. For convenience, in the rest of this paper a VM label denotes the label which is assigned to the dataset that the VM is in. Whenever the VMM allocates one unit of hardware to a VM, which means that a subject requests access to an object, it checks whether the VM label and the hardware's previous access history satisfy the requirement of the access rule.

4   Implementation

The prototype defines a 32-bit integer as a VM label. The first half of 32-bit integer denotes the ID of the dataset in which the VM is. The second half of 32-bit integer denotes the ID of the conflict of interest class to which the VM belongs to. For example a VM label 0x00020004 means that the VM is in the second dataset and belongs to the 4th conflict of interest class. The prototype provides a python script integrated into Xen-tools to assign a label to a VM. The administrator of VMM can issue a command, "xm setcwilabel VM1 0x00020004", to assign the label 0x00020004 to VM1. The label is stored on the VM's configuration file. When starting a VM the VMM loads the VM label from the configuration file and keeps it in the VMM memory for later use.

To enforce the access rule we added some source code into Xen source code. The code alters three kinds of the VMM's behavior. Suppose that there is a VM whose label comprises a dataset ID d and a conflict of interest class ID c_i. Firstly, when the VMM starts the VM and allocates physical CPUs to the VM it checks 32-bit records of all online physical CPUs and the VM label. According to the access rule if and only if an online CPU satisfies a requirement that d_i in its 32-bit record equals d or 0, it can be allocated to the VM. If there are no enough available physical CPUs for the VM, the start operation fails. Secondly, whenever the physical memory allocator of the VMM allocates a physical memory page to the VM, the VMM checks the 32-bit record of the physical memory page and the VM label. According to the access rule if and only d_i in the physical memory page's 32-bit record equals d or 0, this allocation is granted. If the allocation is denied, the physical memory allocator will try to allocate next spare physical memory page to the VM as the same way till there is no available physical memory pages for the VM. Thirdly, when the VMM's CPU scheduler tries to make a virtual CPU (VCPU) migrate from one physical CPU to another physical CPU, the VMM checks the target CPU's 32-bit record and the VM label. According to the access rule if and only d_i in the target CPU's 32-bit record equals d or 0, the VCPU migration is granted.

CWI on I/O adapters which has not been implemented on the prototype also conforms to the access rule.

5   Overheads and Impacts on Security and Resources Utilization

5.1   Overheads

The prototype needs some memory space to keep hardware resources' access histories. The memory overheads for physical CPUs and I/O adapters are very small simply because usually the amount of physical CPUs and I/O adapters in a system is small. But the memory overheads for all physical memory pages are considerable. For example if there is 4GB memory and page size is 4KB, which means that there are 1 million physical memory pages, access histories consume 4MB memory.

We constructed a testbed to test CWI's overheads on the VMM performance. The testbed was built on a Dell server which had 2 1.6 GHz Xeon quad core CPUs and 2 GB DDR2 memory. The testbed used Xen 3.2.1, Debian Linux as the host OS, and Debian XenoLinux as guest OSs. Since VCPU migration is on the critical path while memory and CPUs allocation are not, we measured the computing time increase of SPLASH-2 application programs and the time increase of memory allocation. Because the application programs of SPLASH-2 are CPU-intensive, they are good candidates to test CWI's overhead on VCPU migration. They ran on a guest OS which has 4 VCPUs. We designed 4 test scenarios to measure the computing time increase in detail. The scenario 1 and 3 are that a VM runs on the native VMM. The VM's VCPUs can migrate freely in scenario 1 and are pinned in scenario 3. The scenario 2 and 4 are that a VM runs on the prototype. The VM's VCPUs can migrate freely in scenario 2 and cannot in scenario 4 because of conflict of interest.

In Fig.1 (a), we show that the time of allocating 64 MB or 128 MB memory to the VM often increases by approximate 50%. We define spare memory, which was used by other VMs and cannot be allocated to the VM because of conflict of interest, as contaminated memory. Our test results which are not listed in Fig.1 show the time of allocating 128MB memory behind 64MB contaminated memory to a VM increases by about 10 times since the allocator has to check the 64MB contaminated memory's access histories one by one. But even in such a bad situation the time is less than 1 second. Comparing scenario 1 to scenario 2 we could explore overheads of CWI on successful VCPU migration. And comparing scenario 3 to scenario 4 we could explore overheads of CWI on unsuccessful VCPU migration. In Fig.1 (b) we show that there is a small increase in the computing time of SPLASH-2 application programs with CWI. The increase is 5% on average and the biggest one is 9.1%. Hence based on above results we can safely conclude that overheads of CWI on the VMM performance are very low.

5.2   The Impact on Security

The popularity of multi-core and Hyper-Threading technologies provides new chances to construct covert channels. Popular multi-core processors which have private L1 caches often share L2 caches. C. Percival [8] used an L2 cache-missing approach to build a covert channel between two processes. Zhenghong Wang and Ruby B. Lee [9] used the shared functional units between the insider process and the observer process in a Hyper-Threading processor to effectively build a new kind of covert channels, SMT/FU covert channel. Although these researches didn't focus on virtual machine systems, it is technically feasible to build such kinds of covert channels between two VMs when using multi-core or Hyper-Threading processors. CWI forbids VMs which compete against each other from

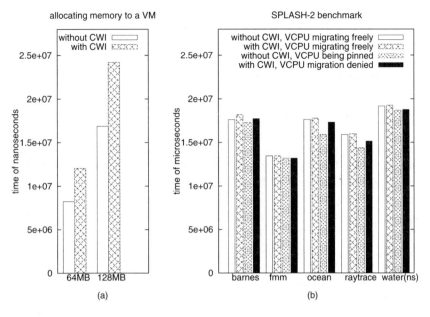

Fig. 1. CWI's overheads on the VMM performance

sharing processors and therefore gets rid of chances to use shared functional units or caches to build covert channels between two VMs.

5.3   The Impact on Hardware Resources Utilization

Both sHype/Xen and PCW model define a whole virtual machine system as one subject. However CWI defines every unit of hardware as one subject. Suppose there are many VMs competing against each other. Only one VM of them can be running on sHype/Xen or PCW at any one time. But many VMs of them can be running on CWI at any one time. It is obvious that compared with other MAC mechanisms CWI improves the hardware resources utilization of virtual machine systems, although it's difficult to do a proper quantitative analysis of the improvement.

6   Conclusion

To improve security of virtual machine systems and take full advantages of virtualization technologies we propose Chinese Wall Isolation mechanism which is based on classical Chinese Wall model. CWI is cost-effective, and makes an air-gap from hardware layer among VMs competing against each other to reduce covert channels. Compared with the native VMM and other related work CWI has two significant advantages as follows. Firstly CWI provides stronger isolation than VMMs do because it keeps more information about relations among

VMs than VMMs do and isolates a VM from other VMs against which the VM competes at hardware layer. By contrast from VMM's perspective VMs are just the same things and basically share all hardware resources. Secondly CWI can get higher hardware resources utilization than other MAC mechanisms like sHype/Xen and PCW model do.

Acknowledgements

This work was supported in part by National Key Basic Research and Development Plan (973 Plan) (No. 2007CB310900), and National Natural Science Foundation of China (No. 90612018 and No. 90715030).

References

[1] Karger, P.A.: Securing virtual machine monitors: what is needed? In: ASIACCS 2009: Proceedings of the 4th International Symposium on Information, Computer, and Communications Security, pp. 1–2. ACM, New York (2009)

[2] Sailer, R., Jaeger, T., Valdez, E., Caceres, R., Perez, R., Berger, S., Griffin, J.L., van Doorn, L.: Building a mac-based security architecture for the xen open-source hypervisor. In: ACSAC 2005: Proceedings of the 21st Annual Computer Security Applications Conference, Washington, DC, USA, pp. 276–285. IEEE Computer Society, Los Alamitos (2005)

[3] Jaeger, T., Sailer, R., Sreenivasan, Y.: Managing the risk of covert information flows in virtual machine systems. In: SACMAT 2007: Proceedings of the 12th ACM symposium on Access control models and technologies, pp. 81–90. ACM, New York (2007)

[4] Brewer, D.F.C., Nash, M.J.: The chinese wall security policy. In: Proceedings of the 1989 IEEE Symposium on Security and Privacy (May 1989)

[5] Barham, P., Dragovic, B., Fraser, K., Hand, S., Harris, T., Ho, A., Neugebauer, R., Pratt, I., Warfield, A.: Xen and the art of virtualization. In: SOSP 2003: Proceedings of the nineteenth ACM symposium on Operating systems principles, pp. 164–177. ACM, New York (2003)

[6] Meushaw, R., Simard, D.: Nettop commercial technology in high assurance applications. Technical report (2000)

[7] Cheng, G., Jin, H., Zou, D., Ohoussou, A.K., Zhao, F.: A prioritized chinese wall model for managing the covert information flows in virtual machine systems. In: ICYCS 2008: Proceedings of the 2008 The 9th International Conference for Young Computer Scientists, Washington, DC, USA, pp. 1481–1487. IEEE Computer Society, Los Alamitos (2008)

[8] Percival, C.: Cache missing for fun and profit. In: BSDCan 2005, Ottawa (2005)

[9] Wang, Z., Lee, R.B.: Covert and side channels due to processor architecture. In: ACSAC 2006: Proceedings of the 22nd Annual Computer Security Applications Conference, Washington, DC, USA, pp. 473–482. IEEE Computer Society, Los Alamitos (2006)

Visualization-Based Study on Information Specification Languages for Network Management Using Formal Concept Analysis

Hui Xu[*] and Debao Xiao

Institute of Computer Network and Communication, Huazhong Normal University
430079 Wuhan, P.R. China
Xuhui_1004@hotmail.com

Abstract. Application of various different management interfaces and protocols leads to urgent requirements of management mediation that introduces management hierarchies, and mediation of management information is the basics for the study on management hierarchy. This paper focuses on examining information specification languages available in network management domain from the viewpoint of information granularity, analyzes the modeling aspects of these languages and discusses their articulation problem based on visualization by means of concept lattices benefited from Formal Concept Analysis. The examples provided in this paper explain how visualization plays a prominent role in studying management information specification languages and their articulation by alignment.

Keywords: Network management; information specification language; visualization; concept lattices; formal concept analysis; articulation.

1 Introduction

Standardization of network management started in the late 1980s, and until now there have been several solutions, the widely adopted one of which is Simple Network Management Protocol (SNMP). And recently, more studies and the industry as well focus on future Internet, three key points of which may be content, service and management [1]. However, SNMP and other existing solutions have limitations of some degree in terms of performance, scalability, flexibility, maintainability and reliability [2], thus don't seem to be quite appropriate for future network management. Note that, application of various different management interfaces and protocols leads to urgent requirements of management mediation, which means the translation between managing and managed systems, introduces management hierarchies and takes place at multiple levels as follows [3].

• Mediation at transport level, which strictly speaking is not really management mediation but only the functionality of a transport gateway that does not involve any translation between the management messages being exchanged.

---

[*] Corresponding author.

L. Boursas et al. (Eds.): SVM 2009, CCIS 71, pp. 19–30, 2010.
© Springer-Verlag Berlin Heidelberg 2010

• Mediation of the management protocol itself, which includes remote operations, management operations and management services.

• Mediation of management information, which is the basics for the study on management hierarchy.

This paper tries to discuss network management information hierarchy from the viewpoint of granularity, which may possibly solve two existing significant problems: a) lack of unification, and b) low level of formalism. In general, network management information hierarchy can be divided into three levels, which are meta-schema, schema and Management Information Base (MIB) instance, as is presented in Fig. 1.

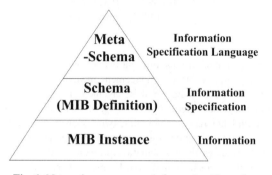

Fig. 1. Network management information hierarchy

As is shown in Fig. 1, the structure of information granularity for network management has been established. Current studies mainly focus on management information and its specification, but rarely on management information specification languages. However, meta-schema (information specification language) is the guideline for schema (MIB definition as information specification), which is then the one for MIB instance (information).

Since the syntax of a management information specification language often reflects its distinctive characteristics in modeling managed objects and their relationships, visualization-based study by means of concept lattices may be a promising way to examine these languages in an integrated way. The aim of this paper is then to analyze these languages for network management information granularity based on visualization using Formal Concept Analysis (FCA, theory of concept lattices).

The remainder of this paper is organized as follows. Related work is discussed in Section 2. And application of FCA techniques is proposed in Section 3, in order to visualize management information languages, with typical examples demonstrated in Section 4. Sequentially in Section 5, articulation problem is further explained based on visualization with the use of concept lattices. Section 6 concludes this paper and prospects future work.

2 Related Work

To the best of our knowledge, few studies have been done on network management information granularity. Reference [4] regards management information specification languages as a term of lightweight ontology because they just define information of the management domain without definition of the axioms or constraints present in heavyweight ontology, which makes them difficult to reason, and compares existing languages in terms of their semantic expressiveness. And since OWL (Web Ontology Language, not an acronym) is a very complete ontology language, it can be directly used to specify management information because it has most of the constructions included in management information specification languages and even those facets that are not included, can be defined by extending OWL and RDFS (Resource Description Framework Schema) [5]. Thus in this way, an OWL ontology may be used as the integration of all management information.

It seems that, researches on this topic are enthusiastic about applying ontology languages to Merge and Map (M&M) management information, but may not take adequate considerations for information granularity. According to the theory of granularity proposed by J. R. Hobbs, the framework for which consists of abstraction, simplification, idealization, articulation and intelligence [6], the crucial features from the environment of network management need to be abstracted, in order to determine an appropriate information granularity. And when shifts in perspective are required, articulation axioms may be used.

3 Applying Formal Concept Analysis to Visualize Management Information Specification Languages

3.1 Proposed Approach

As indicated above, permanent relationships of managed objects are always described by not-lasting terms, such as management information specification languages or OWL. But the fact is that, these terms reflect not only the fashion of the times but also the preferences of the designers or a particular organization. Hence, a more independent study is needed.

Delighted by the thinking of reconstructing a MIB definition as the corresponding MIB tree, we argue that conceptual scheme may be a suitable choice. As one origin of Granular Computing (GrC) [7], concept lattices [8] are an exact mathematic model, essentially reflecting the entity-attribute relationship. And its corresponding Hasse chart can reveal the concept hierarchy. As the theory of concept lattices, FCA is a mathematization of the philosophical understanding of concepts.

In the rest of this section, we will demonstrate how to use concept lattices and FCA techniques for the visualization of different management information specification languages by a unified formalism.

3.2 Unified Formalism Based on Concept Lattices

A formal context for each information specification language in the field of network management can be defined as formal context $K_i = (O_i, A_i, I_i)$, where O_i represents a set of management objects, A_i represents a set of management attributes, and I_i indicates which objects in the set O_i have which attributes in the set A_i. In other words, K_i can be stored as a data sheet that is single-valued.

A formal concept (X,Y) means that a pair of a set of formal objects X (extension that covers all the objects belonging to this concept) and a set of formal attributes Y (intension that involves all the attributes shared by those objects) is closed in a manner, which satisfies the following formula (1) and (2).

$$\{a \in A_i \mid \forall o \in X, oI_i a\} = Y \qquad (1)$$

$$\{o \in O_i \mid \forall a \in Y, oI_i a\} = X \qquad (2)$$

Furthermore, a lattice is a special type of partial order, and it can be viewed as a hierarchical structure where each element may have more than one parent [9]. Thus, partial ordering relations can be described between formal concepts, which are sub-conceptions (defined as $\leq$) and hyper-conceptions (defined as $\geq$), and these two relations are symmetrical in Hasse charts. And a concept lattice is a complete one that has a least upper-bound and a greatest lower-bound [8].

3.3 Application of Formal Concept Analysis for Visualization

Working with management information specification languages seems to become easier with a visual representation, and FCA techniques may possibly be utilized to provide visualization based on concept lattices.

A simple algorithm for the construction of $L(K_i)$ is first to generate all the concepts $\{(X,Y)\}$ contained in K_i and then to determine the concept hierarchy, the key of which is to depict partial ordering relations $\leq$ and $\geq$ for $\{(X,Y)\}$. During this construction process, approaches for reduction of concept lattices may possibly be used to simplify the expression of concept granular in formal context, such as the method of matrix decompositions, in which modified matrix has lower dimensions and acts as input for some known algorithms for lattice construction [10].

Some examples will be provided in the next section to demonstrate the advantages benefited from visualization of concept lattices with the use of FCA techniques.

4   Example Demonstrations

4.1   SMIv2

Originally developed from the similar concept in OSI network management, Structure of Management Information version 2 (SMIv2) [11] is a popular information specification language adopted for computer network management, and it defines organization, composing and identifier used in the framework of SNMP.

Traditionally, SNMP MIB modules (information specifications) are defined by SMIv2. In SMIv2, nine Macros are provided, including MODULE-IDENTITY, OBJECT-IDENTITY, OBJECT-TYPE, NOTIFICATION-TYPE, and so on. For simplicity, we focus on the definitions of module, node, object and notification, which may

```
-- definition for objects
OBJECT-TYPE MACRO ::=
BEGIN
    TYPE NOTATION ::=
                "SYNTAX" Syntax
                UnitsPart
                "MAX-ACCESS" Access
                "STATUS" Status
                "DESCRIPTION" Text
                ReferPart
                IndexPart
                DefValPart

    VALUE NOTATION ::=
                value(VALUE ObjectName)

    ... ...

    UnitsPart ::=
                "UNITS" Text
                | empty

    ......

    ReferPart ::=
                "REFERENCE" Text
                | empty

    IndexPart ::=
                "INDEX" "{" IndexTypes "}"
                | "AUGMENTS" "{" Entry "}"
                | empty

    ......

    DefValPart ::=
                "DEFVAL" "{" Defvalue "}"
                | empty

    ......

END
```

Fig. 2. A brief version of SMIv2 OBJECT-TYPE Macro

be adequately convincing to demonstrate the advantages of applying FCA techniques for visualization of management information specification languages.

First of all, we define module, node, object and notification as formal objects, and abstract formal attributes from their corresponding macro definitions. Take object for example. Fig. 2 shows a brief version of SMIv2 OBJECT-TYPE Macro.

Table 1. Part of formal context for SMIv2

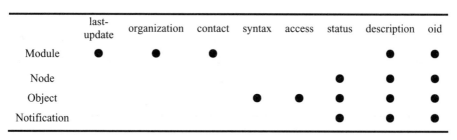

	last-update	organization	contact	syntax	access	status	description	oid
Module	●	●	●				●	●
Node						●	●	●
Object				●	●	●	●	●
Notification						●	●	●

As is presented in Fig. 2, mandatory properties that are syntax, access, status, description and oid are selected as formal attributes, while optional properties that are unit, refer, index and defval are not considered as formal attributes, since they are not necessary for the definition of the corresponding information specification. Thus based on the similar abstraction as above, part of formal context for SMIv2 is provided in Table 1. And Fig. 3 then reveals the corresponding lattice based on the well-known construction algorithms.

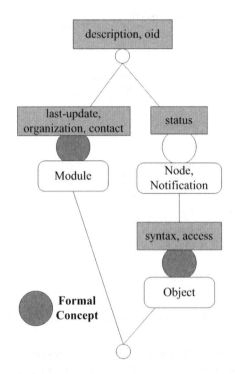

Fig. 3. Lattice generated from part of formal context for SMIv2

Table 2. Part of formal context for SMIng

	revision	organization	contact	object	index	signals	Status	description	oid
Module	●	●	●					●	
Node							●	●	●
Scalars				●			●	●	●
Table				●	●		●	●	●
Notification						●	●		●

4.2 SMIng

Structure of Management Information, next generation (SMIng) [12] [13] is a management information specification language to integrate SMIv2 and Structure of Policy Provisioning Information (SPPI), avoiding the use of ASN.1. As for SMIng, part of its formal context is given in Table 2, and Fig. 4 then presents the corresponding lattice.

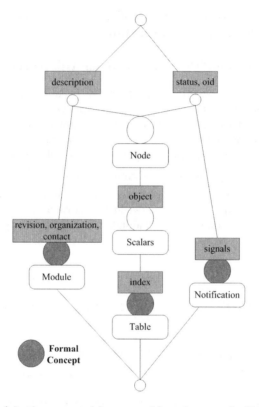

Fig. 4. Lattice generated from part of formal context for SMIng

4.3 Summary

Visualization of a concept lattice is interesting as it makes the information contained in the lattice more accessible [9] and easier to be used in a collaborative environment for humans [14].

On one side, it helps to create hierarchies of objects either merged (such as the term for both node and notification in the SMIv2 lattice shown in Fig. 3) or with clear distinctions (such as two different concepts for table and notification in the SMIng lattice presented in Fig. 4).

On the other side, it promotes convenient modification to the lattice by adding or removing concepts or properties. This advantage can be explored to reuse existing management information specification languages (such as SMIv2 and SMIng) for the design of new languages such as YANG. And in this case, FCA techniques are used to review original languages so as to enhance the understanding of their modeling aspects based on visualization of their concepts and relations. One main advantage of such visualization for the new language design is that when adding a concept name upon the suggestion, properties of the new concept are obvious from the generated lattice [14].

5   Articulation of Management Information Specification Languages Based on Visualization

5.1   Application of Formal Concept Analysis for Articulation

Based on the remarkable benefits of the FCA for visualization by the expression of partial ordering sets, its mathematic formalization can be further applied to the articulation of different management information specification languages.

Designed by different organizations or different thinkings from the same organization, each information specification language for the sake of network management forms a formal context K_i of various attributes that are usually not agreed with any others. Note that, all these formal contexts have a particular attribute area. Fig. 5 shows three relationships available between two attribute areas, which are supplement, overlapping and duplication, and takes available management information specification languages for example.

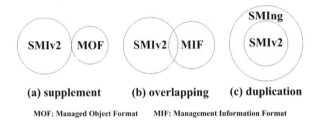

(a) supplement   (b) overlapping   (c) duplication

MOF: Managed Object Format   MIF: Management Information Format

Fig. 5. Examples for three relationships of attribute areas

As for all these three relationships given in Fig. 5, the idea of merging may be used to integrate different management information specification languages, when at the same time mapping is required, since only one fused lattice is produced as a result of the merge process. This has proven to be a difficult task. Thus in this case, the alignment approach for management information specification languages is proposed in favor of articulation. Compared to the merge process, the alignment is a pair of mappings between the source lattices and their articulation.

FCA techniques can then be utilized to provide visualization for articulation of management information specification languages by alignment. On one hand, it promotes the comparison of management information specification languages. On the other hand, it encourages separate analysis of each management information specification language.

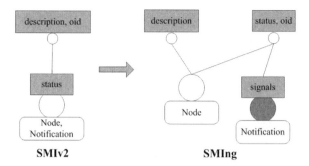

Fig. 6. Evolution analysis of two terms for node and notification based on visualization of concept lattices

5.2 Articulation Analysis Based on Visualization

In order to illustrate articulation analysis benefited from visualization of concept lattices for management information specification languages, we will analyze the evolution from SMIv2 to SMIng as an example.

As is known to most of us, SMIv2 has some drawbacks, which hinder the application of SNMP to manage future networks. And the root lies in the fact that SMI uses a data-oriented approach to model all management aspects. First of all, SMIv2 is insufficient to represent hierarchical network configuration data. Second, SMIv2 is such a conceptually simple language that it is usually quite difficult to be used for modeling complex management operations.

Let's compare the lattice generated from part of formal context for SMIv2 presented in Fig. 3 and the one for SMIng shown in Fig. 4 for a detailed explanation.

(1) According to the visualization of concept lattices, an obvious disadvantage of SMIv2 is that, two terms for object and notification fall into one place. And SMIng lattice adds a distinction in a form that, the term for notification has the property "signals" and the other one does not have, while the term for node has the property "description" and the other one does not have. Fig. 6 demonstrates this evolution.

(2) The concept of SMIv2 object is confusing, since it doesn't make a distinction of scalars and table, which are two different varieties of objects for network management. In SMIng lattice, the concept for object is deleted and the property "object" is added. Two terms for scalars and table are also added, with another property "index" as a distinction. Fig. 7 illustrates this evolution.

(3) Some properties of the formal concept for module are also edited from the SMIv2 lattice to the SMIng lattice. Through visualization, the property "oid" is deleted and the property "last-update" is modified to the property "revision".

From the presentation above, visualization of concept lattices plays an important role in evolution analysis for management information specification languages. Note that, although it was expected that SMIng be an integrated information specification language that could be adapted for different network management protocols, it didn't become a standard language finally, due to the increasing complexity of design when moving towards being a protocol-neutral language. As mentioned above, the new candidate information specification language for network management is YANG [15],

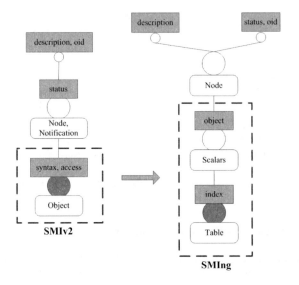

Fig. 7. Evolution analysis from the concept for object to two distinctive terms for scalars and table based on visualization of concept lattices

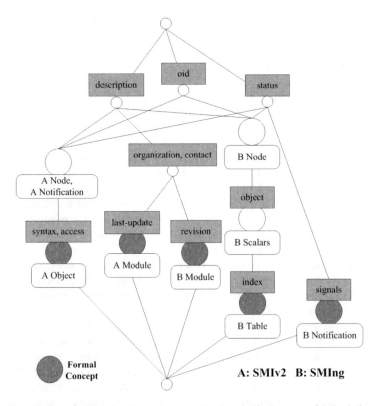

Fig. 8. Hasse diagram by aligning concept lattices in the interest of articulation

which is proposed by Internet Engineering Task Force (IETF) NETCONF Data Modeling Language (netmod) Working Group (WG) [16] and is based on the SMIng syntax. We argue that, visualization of concept lattices for existing management information specification languages may provide some inspiring guidelines for the standardization progress of YANG.

Furthermore, delighted by the method proposed by Reference [17], Fig. 8 provides the Hasse diagram by aligning the lattice generated from part of formal context for SMIv2 presented in Fig. 3 and the one for SMIng shown in Fig. 4 for the purpose of articulation of management information specification languages.

As is implied in Fig. 8, FCA techniques have been exploited to provide visualization by aligning management information specification languages for the purpose of articulation. When comparing different languages, two objects of source lattices are considered as close to each other if they share most of the same attributes, such as the object of module for SMIv2 and the object of module for SMIng. And the lattice resulting from the alignment can also be reused to analyze each source lattice separately, which represents a management information specification language.

6 Conclusions and Future Work

The main contribution of this paper is to discuss management information specification languages from the viewpoint of information granularity, and utilize visualization by means of concept lattices benefited from FCA, in order to discover inner modeling rules of existing information specification languages for the sake of network management and implement their articulation by alignment.

Since this paper only provides a simple example for solving the articulation problem by alignment, future work includes the design of a general alignment method for the articulation of management information specification languages.

Acknowledgments. This work has been supported by the Key Scientific and Technological Project of Hubei Province, P.R. China under Grant No. 2008BAB012, and the Innovation Fund for Graduate Students of Huazhong Normal University.

References

1. Schönwälder, J., Fouquet, M., Rodosek, G.D., Hochstatter, I.C.: Future Internet = Content + Services + Management. IEEE Communication Magazine 47(7), 27–33 (2009)
2. Gupta, A.: Network Management: Current Trends and Future Perspectives. Journal of Network and Systems Management 14(4), 483–491 (2006)
3. Clemm, A.: Network Management Fundamentals. Cisco Press (2006)
4. López de Vergara, J.E., Villagrá, V.A., Asensio, J.I., Berrocal, J.: Ontologies: Giving Semantics to Network Management Models. IEEE Network 17(3), 15–21 (2003)
5. López de Vergara, J.E., Villagrá, V.A., Berrocal, J.: Applying the Web Ontology Language to Management Information Definitions. IEEE Communications Magazine 42(7), 68–74 (2004)
6. Hobbs, J.R.: Granularity. In: Joshi, A.K. (ed.) Proceeding of 9th International Joint Conference on Artificial Intelligence, pp. 432–435 (1985)

7. Yao, Y.Y.: The Art of Granular Computing. In: Kryszkiewicz, M., Peters, J.F., Rybiński, H., Skowron, A. (eds.) RSEISP 2007. LNCS (LNAI), vol. 4585, pp. 101–112. Springer, Heidelberg (2007)
8. Ganter, B., Wille, R.: Formal Concept Analysis: Mathematical Foundations. Springer, Heidelberg (1999)
9. Fabritius, C.V., Madsen, N.L., Clausen, J., Larsen, J.: Finding the Best Visualization of an Ontology. Technical report, Informatics and Mathematical Modelling, Technical University of Denmark (2004)
10. Snasel, V., Abdulla, H.M., Polovincak, M.: Behavior of the Concept Lattice Reduction to Visualizing Data after Using Matrix Decompositions. In: Proceeding of 4th International Conference on Innovations in Information Technology, pp. 392–396. IEEE Press, Los Alamitos (2007)
11. McCloghrie, K., et al. (eds.): Structure of Management Information Version 2 (SMIv2). RFC 2578 (1999)
12. Strauss, F., Schoenwaelder, J.: SMIng - Next Generation Structure of Management Information. RFC 3780 (2004)
13. Strauss, F., Schoenwaelder, J.: Next Generation Structure of Management Information (SMIng) Mappings to the Simple Network Management Protocol (SNMP). RFC 3781 (2004)
14. Obitko, M., Snasel, V., Smid, J.: Ontology Design with Formal Concept Analysis. In: Proceeding of 2004 International Workshop on Concept Lattices and their Applications, pp. 111–119 (2004)
15. Bjorklund, M. (ed.): YANG - A Data Modeling Language for NETCONF. Draft-ietf-netmod-yang-07 (2009) (work in progress)
16. IETF: NETCONF Data Modeling Language Working Group (2009), http://www.ietf.org/html.charters/netmod-charter.html
17. Souza, K., Davis, J.: Aligning Ontologies through Formal Concept Analysis. In: Proceeding of 6th International Conference on Information Integration and Web-Based Applications and Services, pp. 123–132 (2004)

CORSET: Service-Oriented Resource Management System in Linux

Dong-Jae Kang[*], Chei-Yol Kim, and Sung-In Jung

Cloud Computing Research Dept, Software Research Lab, ETRI
138 Gajeongno, Yuseong-gu, Daejeon, Korea
{djkang,gauri,sijung}@etri.re.kr

Abstract. Generally, system resources are not enough for many running services and applications in a system. And services are more important than single process in real world and they have different priority or importance. So each service should be treated with discrimination in aspect of system resources. But administrator can't guarantee the specific service has proper resources in unsettled workload situation because many processes are in race condition. So, we suppose the service-oriented resource management subsystem to resolve upper problems. It guarantees the performance or QoS of the specific service in changeable workload situation by satisfying the minimum resource requirement for the service.

Keywords: Service-oriented, Corset, Resource management, Process group.

1 Introduction

In real business site, the service is more important than single process, because end users will be interested in response time and it is determined by a lot of processes related to the service. So, many related works have been achieved until now to satisfy the requirement, such efforts include Control Group [1], *cpusets, CKRM/ResGroups* [2] and so on. Generally, Service performance will be affected by several system resources, CPU, memory, disk and network I/O bandwidth and each service on the system has different importance in aspect of administrators. So, they should be treated with discrimination. But, we can't make sure that the specific service has the proper resources in unsettled workload situation or higher priority service has more resources than lower priority one because many processes are in race condition and we can't control the situation now. So, we design and implement service-oriented resource management subsystem, CORSET, to resolve the upper described problems and to guarantee the performance or QoS of specific service. CORSET is to provide the service based integrated system resource management to satisfy the minimum resources requirement of services or applications. And it supports the way to control the system resources in service unit with discrimination according to its priority or importance.

---

[*] This work was supported by the IT R&D program of MKE/IITA.
[2008-F-026-02, Development of Linux Kernel for the OSS Platform Enhancement].

L. Boursas et al. (Eds.): SVM 2009, CCIS 71, pp. 31–35, 2010.

2   CORSET Architecture

Fig.1 shows the architecture of CORSET and it consists of four subsystems. As shown in the figure, Resource Controller Subsystem includes the various system resource controllers. They support the process group(service) based allocation and withdrawal of the specific resources, such like CPU, memory, disk bandwidth I/O, network bandwidth I/O and something like that. The resources can be allocated by various policies which limit the maximum usage, guarantee the minimum quantity and divide the total resources by proportion and so on. These policies may be adjusted to each resource controllers differently according to the specific features of them.

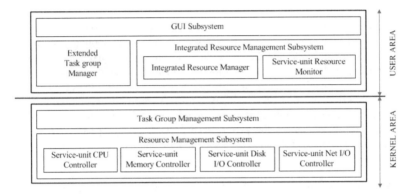

Fig. 1. This is whole architecture of CORSET and it consists of four subsystems

And Task Group Management Subsystem consists of Task Group Manager and Extended Task Group Manager. They provide the primitive functionalities for control of the process groups which mean service. For examples, it creates or deletes a process group and adds or deletes specific process to / from it and move the specific process between them. And this subsystem will be used as framework to add the various resource controllers below it. We use Control Group [1] framework to support upper functionalities. Extended Task Group Manager will support the method for various process grouping. Task Group Manager provides it by only PID, but system administrator may want to do it by name, various attributes, user defined condition and so on. So, it provides the additional grouping options to administrator. Integrated Management Subsystem includes Integrated Resource Manager and Service-unit Resource Monitor to support the advanced resource control functions including automated workload management, condition-based self-configuration and something like that. Basically, this subsystem supports the aggregated and compounded functionalities using the primitive functions supported by lower subsystems as like various resource controllers and Task Group Manager. And it can reduce the administrator's intervention and support management convenience. Service-unit Resource Monitor creates and provides service-unit resource information, for example, current resource usage of service A, current configuration for service B and so on. And it is very important for administrator to recognize the current resource usage by process groups because he/she should know it before adjusts the new configuration to the system. GUI subsystem supports the more convenient and easy management tool for system resources by abstracting the complex interfaces' of below blocks. In next section, we describe the details of specific subsystems focused on Resource Management Subsystem.

3 Service-Oriented Resource Controllers

In this section, we describe the service-oriented resource controllers which are implemented under Task Group Management Subsystem. They control the system resources in service-unit which is supported by upper subsystem. The related works includes CFS, memory controller [4], TC-cgroup, and dm-ioband [3] and so on.

Disk I/O Controller. This controller was implemented as a kind of device mapper driver. So, it is independent of the underlying specific I/O schedulers such like CFQ, AS, NOOP, deadline and so on. And it supports the two kinds of I/O control policies, proportional or predicable I/O bandwidth management. Proportional policy provides the proportional I/O bandwidth, ex. 1:3:5, to process groups based on its priority. And predicable policy supports the range bandwidth, ex. 3M~5M, to the specific process group according to the allocated minimum and maximum bandwidth value of the group. Minimum I/O bandwidth should be guaranteed for stable performance or reliability of specific service and maximum I/O bandwidth should be throttled to protect the limited I/O resource from over-provisioning in unnecessary usage or to reserve the I/O bandwidth for another use. Disk I/O controller uses three criteria, time slice, I/O token and I/O mode to support the control policies. The time slice is a kind of time period for specific service to get the authority of I/O processing. If the time slice is expired, the service will lose its authority for I/O. And I/O Token is used for accounting I/O bandwidth of each service. So, the measuring of the minimum or maximum bandwidth is referred by consumed I/O token. Finally, the I/O mode is a kind of boundary that makes a change of scheduling condition and it is altered based on the consumed I/O token. If it is changed, different scheduling condition and time slice sharing policy will be selected for each I/O mode. Proportional policy uses only I/O token and predicable one includes all.

Network I/O Controller. Network I/O controller uses the existing TC, Traffic Control, module in linux kernel. TC already supports many functions to satisfy the requirements of CORSET, such as bandwidth guaranteeing or limitation and fixed bandwidth. But, TC has some problems that can't recognize a process group. Therefore, it can't control network traffic according to the process group. So, we design and implement the related parts into the controller which assign the group identity to each process group and makes TC to recognize it for traffic control in group unit. When a socket is created, network I/O controller takes the identity of process group which socket creator is on and adds the identity information into the socket. And, in case that creator process is moved to another process group network controller make all sockets by the creator to move into same process group. With the functions, when a socket sends data, the specific group including it is attached to the data packet. TC recognizes the identity in each packet and decides how it is controlled as like pass, hold or drop.

CPU and Memory Controller. The functionalities for group based control of CPU and memory are already supported in linux kernel mainline. So, we used existing CFS for CPU controller and memory resource controller [4] for memory controller in CORSET. Therefore, we describe it briefly in this section. Memory controller supports the allocation of fixed-size memory to a process group. And it isolates the memory behavior of a process group from the rest of the system. The core of the design is to track the current memory usage and limit of the group of processes associated with the controller. Currently, it enables control of both RSS and page cache through providing a double LRU. Global memory pressure causes reclaim from the global LRU and a process group on hitting a limit reclaims from its own LRU. CPU controller supports the proportional share of existing CPU power among process groups. At present, there are two mechanisms to support process group for CPU bandwidth control, user identity and process group identity. The former is to assemble processes into a group according to user id and the latter is to use process group by Control Group framework. CPU bandwidth between two process groups can be divided in the ratio of their CPU shares set by administrator. For example, administrator enables group A to get twice the bandwidth of group B.

4   Experimental Evaluation and Concluding Remarks

In this section, we evaluated the service-oriented resource controllers, focused on disk and network I/O controllers. We don't treat the CPU and memory controllers here, but you can refer the related information in these references [4].

Table 1. Hardware and software system specification for the evaluation

| | Evaluation System Specification (H/W & S/W) | | | | | |
	System	OS	Disk	CPU	Mem	Tools
Spec	SAMSUNG Smart Server ZSS108	linux (kernel-2.6.30-rc1)	SAMSUNG SATA-2, 7,200rpm, 80G	1-way, Intel Pentium4 3.4 GHz	2 GB	fio-1.26 netperf-2.4.1

Table 1 shows evaluation environment for test. And Fig. 2 shows the I/O bandwidth control by disk and network controllers. We create three process groups, grp1, grp2, grp3, for each controller and ran the five workloaders, fio is for disk and netperf is for network controller, in each group. As showed in Fig. 2, proportional share is to allocate I/O bandwidth according to the defined ratio of total bandwidth and predicable and fixed share is to guarantee the expectable bandwidth which one want to allocate regardless of whole bandwidth. Of course, defined ratio and predicable weight is related with priority of the group.

In this paper, we supposed service-oriented resource management system to guarantee the performance or QoS of a specific service in unsettled or unexpected workload situation. It provides the convenient environment for service-unit resource management according to priority or weight of the service. The feature enables the administrator to support the reasonable and expectable system resource to each

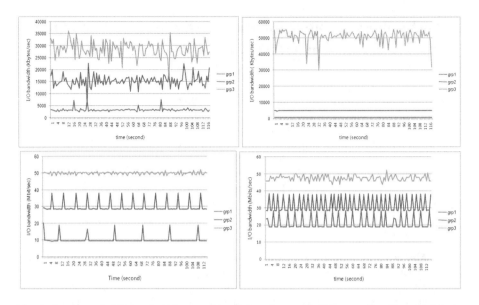

Fig. 2. Service-unit I/O bandwidth control by disk and network I/O controller. Upper-left is for proportional allocation (grp1:grp2:grp3=1:5:9) and upper-right is for predicable allocation (grp1:0.5~0.7Mbytes, grp2:3~5Mbytes, grp3:50~55Mbytes) by disk controller. And lower-left is fixed allocation (grp1:10Mbits/sec, grp2:30Mits/sec, grp3:50Mbits/sec) and lower-right is for minimum guaranteeing (grp1:10+Mbits/sec, grp2:20+Mits/sec, grp3:30+Mbits/sec) by network I/O controller.

service. And it makes the limited I/O resource to be used efficiently and to be controlled dynamically and freely according to the priority of the focused service. So, it can be meaningful in stable performance of the specific application or service.

References

1. Menage, P.B.: Adding Generic Process Containers to the Linux Kernel. In: Proceedings of the Linux Symposium, vol. 2, pp. 45–57 (2007)
2. Nagar, S., Franke, H., Choi, J., Seetharaman, C., Kaplan, S., Singhvi, N., kashyap, V., Smith, M.K.: Class-based Prioritized Resource Control in Linux. In: Proceedings of the Linux Symposium, pp. 150–168 (2003)
3. Tsuruta, R., Kang, D.-J.: Linux Block I/O Bandwidth Control,
   http://sourceforge.net/projects/ioband/
4. Jonathan, C.: Memory Use Controller Documentation,
   http://lwn.net/Articles/268937/

A Technology Explore for the Content-Based Web Query Service on MODIS Level 1B Products

Dong Yan[1], Haibo Liu[2], and Jianzhong Zhou[1]

[1] College of Hydropower & Information Engineering,
Huazhong University of Science & Technology, Luoyu Road. 1037,
430074 Wuhan, China
[2] Institute of Seismology China Earthquake administration, Hongshance Road. 40,
430071 Wuhan, China
freezeday@163.com, liuhb@eqhb.gov.cn, prof.zhou.hust@263.net

Abstract. Query basing on content and geographical scope can increase the MODIS 1B data retrieval efficiency significantly. This article explores how to achieve the content-based web query service. The roadmap includes preprocessing the data to generate additional and assistant information for content-based query, relational database designed for storing the information, the work flow of content-based web query, display of query results and data transfer. Relevant technical key points are also discussed in detail. This roadmap adapts to some utilization specificities of the remote sensing data, and it is a good base to estimate a content-based query of more universality.

Keywords: content-based query; MODIS; web service.

1 Introduction

MODIS is a remote sensor on terra and aqua satellites. Many countries are receiving and using the MODIS data. At present, the distributed data in China is MODIS level 1B products.

In the preview and retrieval of products, the common used methods are snapshot view and file name based management[1][2]on the website. In this way, we can check every image and find the files fully meet the requirements when the amount of data is little. But when we face large amount of data, the efficiency of snapshot view and file name based query is extremely low. A considerable part of the level 1B files found by the file name based retrieval is useless to the user because the study area is covered by cloud. If there are too many files, it is impossible for the users to check every snapshot view and then the useless files can not be excluded. As for the useful files, there is also a considerable part of content whose territory is out of study area and is useless, either.

Because the level 1B products are distributed in the form of integer, much of the download time for the files is wasted on the useless information. Obviously, if we can make query basing on the data content and geographical scope, the retrieval efficiency will be increased and the time for data transfer will be cut down significantly.

L. Boursas et al. (Eds.): SVM 2009, CCIS 71, pp. 36–42, 2010.

The Institute of Hydropower and Digital Engineering in Huazhong University of Science and Technology has the capability of MODIS data reception and also face some problems in using and managing the mass data. Every day the data is burned on DVD and then the digital discs are numbered. When someone wants to use the data, the only way is to check all discs in the study period and it is a very laborious and time-consuming work.

The mass data management is difficult and relevant studies focus on how to make catalogue[3] or how to use existing spatial database soft[4][5] like Oracle Spatial. So we are trying to make efficient query and utilization on mass MODIS data in a different way. This article is an introduction to the technology roadmap of our work.

2 Technical Roadmap

Making direct content-based query on the images when we need data requires powerful processing capability of computer server and the efficiency is low. Taking this into account, the guideline of our work is to make additional preparation for every image and the query is implemented not on the images but on the results of preparation.

The cloud cover is a key to whether the data of one area is useful to the regular users. So we preprocess the level 1B products firstly to generate the data set which could show which part of the image is covered by cloud. Then we import the data set into a relational database and the content-based query is implemented in the database using SQL orders. The results will be shown in web page using simple graphics. Finally, we extract the useful part from the level 1B products according to the requirements of users and transfer the extracted data to the user.

2.1 Preprocessing

After the common correction like bowtie correction, the preprocessing of MODIS 1B products will generate the non-cloud covered or cloud covered region of the MODIS image. If we check every pixel of the image, the information about cloud cover will be complete. But the data amount of result is large and the complete information isn't necessary because we only need to know the general situation of the image. Thus, we generate information about the cloud covered area with a lower resolution to get smaller data amount.

First, we make an integer judgment for the product file to know whether most of the area in the image is covered by cloud. If cloud coverage ratio is greater than 50%, we will record the location of non-cloud covered area, and if coverage ratio is less than 50%, we will record the location of the cloud covered area.

The integer judgment method is to resample the whole MODIS image. According to the pre-defined quantity and spatial distribution of resampling points, we check whether these points are covered by cloud. Here we assume that the cloud coverage ratio of resampling points is equal to that of the whole product file.

After the judgment, we resample the whole product file in a lower resolution. Different to the first resample, this time we use resampling grid which include numbers of pixels. The resolution is also defined with the resampling grid. In the resampling, if a grid is judged as non-cloud covered, we choose to or not to preserve the spatial information of the grid according to the previous judgment. In the grid judgment, we also set a standard value: 50%. Only when the non-clouded cover ratio of the grid is larger than the standard value, the grid is identified as non-cloud covered.

Then, we get the data set including two-dimensional array and auxiliary information after resampling. The two-dimensional array records the longitude and latitude of the grid, the auxiliary information records the product file acquisition time, integer judgment result of the product file, the cover area of the product file and which satellite produced the file. We use the standard of MODIS 1B product file to record the file acquisition time and the satellite.

The preprocessing will be established as an individual function module and will be set up in our MODIS data receiving system. When an image is downloaded from the satellite, the preprocessing module will be activated immediately to generate the data set, and then record the results in the relational database.

2.2 Relational Database

The data set produced by the preprocessing is imported into a relational database. We build two tables to store the data set. They are product file table and area table.

The product file table records the auxiliary information. It has eleven fields. The first three fields are acquisition time (date type), satellite (string type) and judgment (integer type). The other eight fields record the location of the four corner points of the MODIS image. They are the longitude of northwest point (string type), the latitude of northwest point (string type), the longitude of southwest point (string type), the latitude of southwest point (string type), the longitude of southeast point (string type), the latitude of southeast point (string type), the longitude of northeast point (string type) and the latitude of northeast point (string type). In the judgment field, we use "0" and "1" to present the non-cloud and cloud covered area. Using the judgment field, we can know the general situation of cloud cover. With the acquisition time field, we can know how many files generated during the study area. We can also find which files include the study area by making a judgment on whether one corner point of the MODIS image locates in the study area.

The area table records the array of geographical coordinates in the data set. The table has four fields. They are grid longitude (string type), grid latitude (string type), acquisition time (date type) and satellite (string type). The acquisition time and satellite fields of the product file table are the foreign objects of the area table. Combining the area table to the value of judgment field in product file table, we can know whether the grid presents the cloud covered area or non-cloud covered area.

In the MODIS 1B standard, the acquisition time is represented with a string code. In the data set storing, the string code needs to be transferred to the date type. It is indispensable for the query.

2.3 Content-Based Query

The query is a web-based server and the relational database is the object of the query basing on content and the geographical scope.

The geographical scope and the study period are imported by the user in the web page. Then the server generates relevant SQL orders and transfers the orders to the database. Here the SQL orders have two levels.

The first level SQL order searches the product file table firstly to find which files cover the whole or part geographical scope and relevant acquisition time is in the study period. Then we generate two kinds of second level SQL order according to the value of the judgment field of the records matching the spatial and temporal requirements.

For the grids representing non-cloud covered area, the second level SQL order will make search in the area table directly. For the grids representing cloud covered area, the second level SQL order will make searches both in the product file table and in the area table. It means that the spatial information about cloud covered grids need to be transferred to represent the non-cloud covered grids according to the area scope stored in the longitude and latitude fields of the product file table.

The longitude and latitude information from the area table searched out by the second level SQL order are the results of the query. After the server receive these results, it can draw a picture in the web page to show the spatial information for every product file search out by the first level SQL order, just like the snapshot view. The spatial border of the picture is just the imported geographical scope. The picture only has three colors, for example, black, white and grey. The black represents the non-clouded area; the white is on the contrary; the grey represents the area without any data (the covered area of one product file may not include the whole study area). For each picture, only the area in black color is the search results of the second level SQL order, and the area in white and gray color is auto filled by the system. Through the simply pictures, the user will know which MODIS 1B product files match his requirements better.

In this way, some pictures may be mostly or totally covered by the color representing the cloud. From the viewpoint of convenience and efficiency, it is necessary to avoid this situation. So we will provide a function for the user to define a standard value. Only when the non-clouded cover ratio of the study area is larger than the standard value, the relevant results will be shown in the wed page. Obviously, the corresponding SQL orders will be much more complicated.

2.4 Data Transfer

When the user select the pictures in the web page and request to download relevant MODIS 1B product files, we will generate the original MODIS 1B product file names. Subsequently, we extract the content of selected spatial scope from the original product files using the interface functions and build a new MODIS 1B product file for every original product file. The new files are as same as the original files except the geographical scope of coverage. For most studies, the spatial scope of study area is much smaller than the scope of original product file, so the data amount needs to be transferred to the user is reduced significantly and transfer time will also be cut down clearly comparing to transferring the whole original product file.

Instant data transferring needs mass data storage device like disk array. The investment is big and if we can't afford the storage device, we'll only develop relevant algorithm and the data transfer in real system may be a demonstration function. It means that only a part of MODIS 1B product files can be downloaded through the web.

3 Key Points

In the roadmap, there are several technical key points for the successful query.

3.1 Integer and Grid Judgment

In the integer and grid judgment of preprocessing, we focus on how many resampling points are appropriate and how to distribute the points to reflect the overall situation of cloud cover in product file and resampling grid. Because the integer and grid judgment aren't an instant operation, the effect of relevant arithmetic is most important and the time for processing is the secondary requirement.

3.2 Scale of Resampling Grid

Obviously, smaller scale of resampling grid will produce more complete cloud cover information and make better visualization effect of pictures. But the amount of data set will increase and the speed of query will decrease with the higher resolution. So we will compare the resampling speed, data amount, query speed and the visualization effect with different spatial scale of resampling grid. The query speed and the visualization effect are more important. The former is related to the instant operation and experience of user; the latter is related to whether the user could have clear understanding of the simple pictures in web pages. According to the test results, we'll choose a compromise scale to get a balance between query speed and effect.

3.3 Data Set Record

Now we record the cloud cover information one grid by one grid in the area table. This method is easy and is convenient to query. But if we want to record continuous non-cloud or cloud covered area, the method is of low efficiency in data storage. The optional methods include recording the locations of start grid and the end grid, or recording the location of start grid and the numbers of grids following the start grid in line or row.

If we change the recording method, the logic of SQL orders may be more complicated. So we will test different recording methods to get a balance between data storage and query speed. The area table structure in relational database may be adjusted according to the test results.

3.4 Wave Bands

The cloud cover area needs to be excluded for some specific usage, but for other aspects, the cloud cover is no longer a dominative factor. In fact, the dominative factor changes in different wave band and it is the focus of further study.

In addition, when the server generates the new MODIS 1B product files for the users, we hope we can afford a function with which the users can select the wave bands included in the new file. Every wave band is useful only for some specific functions and some wave bands are definitely useless in a certain study. The data transfer time will be cut down further if we exclude the useless wave bands out of the new file. To achieve this purpose, we need comprehensive and deep understanding of the product file format and corresponding interfaces.

3.5 ChinaGrid and Distributed Computing

The Institute of Hydropower and Digital Engineering has a set of HP cluster computer which has been included in the ChinaGrid developed by the Ministry of Education of the People's Republic of China. By virtue of this cluster computer, we can improve the capability of the content-based query server for current and future mass data of different sensors and make it possible for improving the query server to a new function of the image processing grid in the ChinaGrid. So, the distributed computing will be concerned in every phase of the study.

3.6 Expansibility

Current roadmap is based on the identification of cloud cover. If we can identify more information, the content-based query will have more practical significance.

The MODIS data is widely used in research of atmosphere, land surface temperature, vegetation, fire control and other aspects. Every study needs to identify the meaning of the pixel in some wave band. These interpretations are difficult but the results are very valuable references to future work. Today the results of interpretation are stored in separate institutions and individuals; they are difficult to be shared. If we can share the results from different research aspects, the interdisciplinary integration may be much easier.

In the study, we will try to import the interpretation result of MODIS image into the query. New preprocessing needs to be set up and relational table should be adjusted according to the features of different interpretations.

In the preprocessing, the integer judgment will be removed because we must record the interpretation of all non-cloud covered area. The resampling grid is still necessary to make the scale of interpretation match the standard. The judgment about resampling grids should be improved to identify the main or all types of the interpretation results of the area in the grid. We'll get the data set with additional interpretation information, and then store the interpretation information in a new added field in the area table. Different serial number will be used to represent variant types of interpretation results. In the product file table we'll also add a new field in which "0" and "1" are used to discriminate whether the relevant file is an original MODIS 1B product file.

When we show the results of interpretation-based query in the web page, the simple picture of three colors isn't efficient enough to show the variant information and then the colorful image is essential. The color will auto-generated according predefined standard and then every image will have its own legend.

In addition, the interpretation about some MODIS images may come from different institution and individuals. As a result, the formats of relevant files may be different to each other, which will increase the complexity of data preprocessing and transfer.

4 Conclusion

Content-based image query is the developing trend and has great potential applications. Our work is a test to the content-based query in remote sensing image. The roadmap indeed is to build auxiliary information for the query. This design adapts to some utilization specificities of the remote sensing data, but it isn't a universal method. The expansibility study may be a chance to estimate the method of more universality.

References

1. Qian, J., Zheng, X.: The Satellite Data Archive System of National Satellite Meteorological Center. Journal of Applied Meteorological Science 14, 756–762 (2003)
2. Chen, B., Chen, Z.: Research on Archive Method of Massive Remote Sensing Data. Remote Sensing Information 21, 43–46 (2006)
3. Wang, C., Tang, L.: Discussion on Compatibility of Satellite Data Catalogue and Archive System. Remote Sensing Technology and Application 22, 428–432 (2007)
4. Wang, X.: Study on the Architecture and Application Pattern of Oracle Spatial 10g Geo-Raster. Remote Sensing Technology and Application 21, 468–472 (2006)
5. Wang, L., Wu, Y.: The Technology of Storing Remote Images Based on Oracle Database. Journal of Institute of Surveying and Mapping 19, 258–261 (2002)

CFCC: A Covert Flows Confinement Mechanism for Virtual Machine Coalitions

Ge Cheng, Hai Jin, Deqing Zou, Lei Shi, and Alex K. Ohoussou

Services Computing Technology and System Lab
Cluster and Grid Computing Lab
School of Computer Science and Technology
Huazhong University of Science and Technology, Wuhan, 430074, China
{Hjin,deqingzhou}@hust.edu.cn, chengge@xtu.edu.cn,
foxshee@yahoo.com.cn, ohouss@hotmail.com

Abstract. Normally, virtualization technology is adopted to construct the infrastructure of cloud computing environment. Resources are managed and organized dynamically through virtual machine (VM) coalitions in accordance with the requirements of applications. Enforcing mandatory access control (MAC) on the VM coalitions will greatly improve the security of VM-based cloud computing. However, the existing MAC models lack the mechanism to confine the covert flows and are hard to eliminate the convert channels. In this paper, we propose a covert flows confinement mechanism for virtual machine coalitions (CFCC), which introduces dynamic conflicts of interest based on the activity history of VMs, each of which is attached with a label. The proposed mechanism can be used to confine the covert flows between VMs in different coalitions. We implement a prototype system, evaluate its performance, and show that our mechanism is practical.

Keywords: cloud computing, covert flows confinement, virtual machine coalition, mandatory access control.

1 Introduction

Virtualization technology is becoming more and more popular in cloud computing [1][2] environment, such as Elastic Compute Cloud of Amazon, Blue Cloud of IBM. Cloud computing greatly changes the usage mode of traditional computing resources. The enterprises/organizations need not to keep purchasing expensive hardware resources to satisfy their growing computing or storage requirement and spending much money to maintain the computer systems. Data center [3], a popular cloud computing application, possesses huge computing and storage resources, which gives cloud users the illusion of infinite computing and storage resources available on demand. So it is natural that resources in cloud computing environment are allocated in VM granularity for cloud users and VMs are isolated from each other. Multiple VMs belonging to one cloud user are located in different hardware nodes, which constitute a VM coalition.

L. Boursas et al. (Eds.): SVM 2009, CCIS 71, pp. 43–54, 2010.
© Springer-Verlag Berlin Heidelberg 2010

Although multiple VMs and their workloads on the same hardware platform offer great benefits, it also raises the risk of information leakage between workloads belonging to different companies which may compete with each other. Enforcing MAC between VMs provides an attractive mechanism to improve the security of VM based cloud computing. Dynamic coalitions [4], also called domains in some papers, are used to organize VMs over nodes, and security policies differ in each coalition normally.

There are many VM coalition building approaches, which have been proposed in distributed VM systems, such as NetTop [5], Shamon [6], and Trusted Virtual Domain [7][8]. Enforcing mandatory access control on the distributed VM systems can provide secure information operations. Even with MAC enforcement, information involving possible conflicts of interest may be exchanged between nodes, such as sensitive information related to enterprise/organization trade secrets. For example, Information from a VM with workload of competitors should be handled safely without mixing and improper flows of information by building coalitions for VMs with different companies' workload. However the existing MAC models cannot eliminate covert channel [9], which is a mechanism not explicitly designed for communication between parties. For example, if both two parties have the access to a disk, they may use it as a covert channel by controlling the exhaustion of the disk's storage space. Although overt communication channels are enforced by explicit authorizations and we have some tools to check comprehensive coverage of authorizations to these channels [10] [11], covert channels are difficult to identify and perhaps impossible to eliminate completely.

However, a policy in terms of overt communication channels does not enable the management of the risk caused by covert channels. The reason is that any VM on the system may be able to communicate with any other VM through the covert channel. For example, when a distributed system based on VM coalition loads a VM, a covert channel may exist because the VM maybe leaks information in an implicit way to another VM in the same node.

Some policies [12] [13] are proposed to manage the risk of covert flows and they are added to the MAC policies as confinement conditions for covert flows. However, such policies lead to the cost of increasing complexity and decreasing performance. The policies also need the overall system history and lack the enforcement algorithms. Furthermore the distributed systems based on VM coalition lack the mechanism to record the history and current overall system state to enforce those policies.

To address the above questions, in this paper, we propose a covert flows confinement mechanism for VM coalitions (CFCC) in VM-based cloud computing. CFCC can minimize the impact on the usability, which uses the combination of the policy control center and distributed reference monitors[1] to implement a Trusted Computing Base (TCB).

CFCC aims that managing the covert flows is not to eliminate covert channels by rewriting hypervisor code in each node but to prevent the covert flows through fine-grained resource management, and to enable users to mitigate the impact of remaining covert channels when necessary. CFCC uses an effective but simplified alternative of the prioritized Chinese-Wall model[12], with a mandatory access control mechanism

---

[1] Each physical machine has a reference monitor capable of enforcing MAC policies over its VMs.

for all communication, migration, startup of VMs without changing current MAC policies inside the coalitions. Both the subjects and objects of the Chinese-Wall policies are VMs. A label defined by the system administrator is attached to a VM, and the information flows between label-attached VMs will be controlled. We implemented a prototype system, and show that the covert flows can be dealt with safety even when conflicts of interest occur. In addition, we measured the performance overhead to show that our mechanism is practical.

The rest of this paper is organized as follows: related work is discussed in Section 2; in Section 3, we describe the design of CFCC. Section 4 gives an implementation of CFCC and evaluates our prototype system. Finally, we conclude and discuss future work in Section 5.

2 Related Work

SHype security architecture [4] adds authorization control to Xen's overt communication mechanisms to authorize inter-VM communication on the same machine. Shamon [6], a system on the Xen hypervisor with a trusted MAC virtual machine, implements the MAC policy at two software layers: the Xen hypervisor (sHype MAC in Xen) that controls inter-VM resource accesses, and SELinux and IPsec network controls. Each of these systems uses a Type Enforcement model [14] to describe inter-VM communications that are authorized in a system. However, authorization of inter-VM communications can only manage information flows through an overt channel, but cannot control information flows through a covert channel. sHype and Shamon didn't consider complicated covert channels. For example, if there are several intermediates among two communication parties, a complicated covert channel may exist.

NetTop [5] isolates user execution environments from the host OS by VMware, and allows connecting the confined environments to each other to form a network of trusted environments. NetTop takes the host OS and VMware as TCB, and uses a secure OS such as SELinux to increase the security level of TCB.

The European Multilaterally Secure Computing Base [15] is a secure computing platform to enable multilateral security by combining Trusted Computing Group technology for trusted computing and micro-kernel-based virtualization technologies. It is focusing on the development of infrastructures for enterprise rights management.

The Trusted Virtual Domain (TVD) integrates virtualization-based security and system management to provide trust and containment guarantees to the data center environment, which is a combination with previous work on trusted computing [16], virtual TPM [17], trust measurement architecture [18] [19], and sHype mandatory access control extensions to the Xen [21] and PHYP [20] hypervisors. TVD [7][8] aims to simplify user and administration interactions on large-scale systems by uploading the security enforcement onto the infrastructure.

Some policies [12] [13] have been developed to manage the covert information flows in VM systems. Those models express the accepted risk of covert data leakage in VM systems. The risk flows policies can be expressed by other access control models, such as Caernarvon [22] that expresses the range of the access, the Chinese-Wall policy [23] and modified Chinese-Wall policy [12] that express the constraint of information flows. Those policies are almost history-based, which needs to have the knowledge of the current system state to make decisions. The current system state can be considered to encompass the history of the system and require great coordination among the decision-making modules in all nodes.

3 Design of CFCC

The primary goal of this paper focuses on covert flows confinement between VM coalitions. We use the Chinese-Wall policy to describe the conflicts of interest to meet the requirement of covert flows confinement between two coalitions. The follows are the requirement of covert flows confinement: 1) covert information flows between label-attached VMs whose labels are the same are permitted; 2) covert information flows between label-attached VMs whose labels belong to different conflicts of interest are permitted; 3) covert information flows between label-free VMs are permitted; 4) covert information flows between label-attached VMs whose labels belong to the same conflicts of interest are disallowed.

To satisfy these requirements, two features are needed in our architecture: distributed mandatory access control for all VMs and centralized information exchange. Both need to be implemented simultaneously based on the activity history of VMs.

3.1 CFCC Architecture

The architecture of our design is shown in Figure 1, in which the covert flows confinement faction consists of two modules: policy management module and policy enforcement module. A policy management module is located in a specific node named Overall Security Server (OSS) acting as policy center, and other policy management modules are located in Local Security Servers (LSS) of other nodes. A Security Network communication channel, such as IPSec, is established between the OSS and a LSS. The specific OSS, policy center, aims to offer an overall view of the system by recording the running history of VMs including VMs start, communication and migration. LSSes need to cache some extra VM coalition information from the OSS besides local policies. The VM coalition information cached by a LSS includes VM start, VM migration and communication history among VMs related to the local node and can be synchronized between the LSS and the OSS once the information

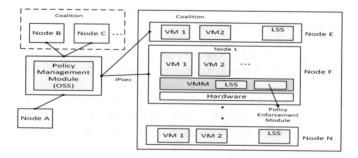

Fig. 1. System architecture of CFCC

changes. The communication for system state synchronization could be done by the Security Network communication channels between the OSS and LSSes, using either regular update method or driving update method.

The policies used by the OSS and LSSes adopt XML specification, which could simplify the policy creation process and make the policies easy to understand. The Security Network communication channels are implemented via MAC-labeled IPSec tunnels.

Policy enforcement in the system is done by a policy enforcement module which is located in the hypervisor of each node. The module consists of a control function and an enforcement function. The task of the control function is to make decisions based on current system information, to interact with a LSS to establish a security policy, and to trigger callback function to deliver policy decisions to the enforcement function. Then the enforcement function uses the policy decisions to control the behaviors of VMs, including VM start, close, migration, and communications among VMs. The control function stores all access control decisions locally to support the enforcement function. No matter what type of decision, it needs to be delivered to the enforcement function.

In our architecture, the OSS plays a role of a policy center and each LSS needs to register to the OSS before it starts up. After registration, the LSS has to precede a synchronization process to download global and local policies, and build the entire access control enforcement environment. When a new node adds, a strict but simple inspection process will be set up to examine if the node configures with a complete LSS & policy enforcement module. Once the node passes through the examination, a security network communication channel will be constructed between the OSS and the new-coming LSS. Then a new node has been added into the whole system and under the control of the OSS.

3.2 Covert Flows Confinement

We use the Chinese-Wall Type Label and Conflict of Interest Set (CIS) to describe the requirement of covert flows confinement between VM coalitions. For example, assuming there are four Chinese-Wall labels, including T1, T2, T3, and T4, if we want to ensure that covert flows cannot exist between VMs with label T1 and VMs with label T3, or between VMs with label T1 and VMs with label T4, we can define that T1 and T3, T1 and T4 belong to a conflict of interest set. We note that the conflict relationship is symmetrical, that is, if T1 conflicts with T3, T3 also conflicts with T1. However, the conflict relationship is not usually reflexive and transitive. We can denote the conflict of interest set as CIS: {(T1, T3) (T1, T4)}.

We know that the label of the Chinese-Wall policy is used for VMs, and VMs with the same label constitute a coalition. Label-free VMs or label-attached VMs whose labels belong to different conflict of interest sets cannot run concurrently with the label-attached VMs which don't join the same coalition with the frontal VMs. Then they will build a new coalition in which labels of VMs will have the same conflict of interest set. For example, T3 and T2 have no conflict of interest, so T2 can join the coalition of T3, which means that T2 can run concurrently or communicate with T3, and then T2 will be in conflict with T1 according to the above CIS. There may be many VM coalitions in the system, we use a History Chinese-Wall Type Array

(HCWTA) to record the labels in the same coalition. As all the VMs in a node belong to a coalition, each node has a HCWTA. The Overall Security Server (OSS) collects all HCWTAs of VM coalitions and builds a table named History Chinese-Wall Types Table (HCWTT). Before system initialization, HCWTA of each node and HCWTT of overall Security Server (OSS) are both empty.

The algorithm of VMs start is used to determine whether the VM with label T1 starting in node N1 (we use HCWTA1 to denote HCWTA of node N1) is allowed or not. The LSS of node N1 needs to communicate with the OSS, and gets the entire labels in the same coalition with the VMs running in this node, which is used for the LSS to infer whether there are covert flows between two VMs whose labels are a conflict of interest belonging to the CIS, when the VM with label T1 starts on node N1.

```
Procedure Algorithm of VMs start
  If (HCWTA1 is empty) {
    A VM is permitted to start in a local node;
    Put the VM's label in HCWTA1 of the local node;
    Update the HCWTA1-related item of HCWTT in the OSS;
  }
  else {
    Update HCWTA1 according to HCWTT in the OSS;
    Lock the HCWTA1-related item of HCWTT in the OSS;
    if (the VM's label is in HCWTA1 ){
    The VM is permitted to start;
    }
      else if (The VM's label is not in conflict with
            the labels listed in HCWTA1 ) {
        The VM is permitted to start in the node;
        Put the VM label in HCWTA1 of the local node;
        Update the HCWTA1-related item of HCWTT in the
        OSS;
      }
      else{
        The VM start requirement is denied;
      }
        Unlock the HCWTA1-related item of HCWTT in the
OSS;
  }
 end procedure
```

The algorithm of VM migration and communication is used for determining whether the requirement of communication and migration between nodes is allowed or not. We make two assumptions for the algorithm: 1) there are two nodes N1 and N2 and their history Chinese-Wall arrays are HCWTA1and HCWTA2; 2) there is a VM in node N1 which wants to communicate with the VM in node N2 or a VM in node N1 which wants to be migrated to node N2. The algorithm of VM migration and communication shows the process of determining whether the requirement of VM migration or communication is permitted or not, which is similar to the VM start algorithm. All the label information in the coalition is needed to determine whether VM communication and migration will produce the covert flows between VMs whose labels are a conflict of interest belonging to the CIS.

```
Procedure Algorithm of VM migration and communication
   Update HCWTA1 and HCWTA2 according to the
   corresponding items of HCWTT in the OSS;
   Lock the items of HCWTT in the OSS;
   if (HCWTA1 == HCWTA2){
     Permit the VM communication or migration
     requirement;
   }
   else{
      if( T ∈HCWTA1,T∈∪{CIS(x)|x∈HCWTA2}) {
      Deny the VM communication or migration
      requirement;
   }
     else {
        Permit the VM communication or migration
        requirement;
        Update the values of both the two items of HCWTT
        in the OSS as HCWTA1∪HCWTA2
        Update the values of both HCWTA1 and HCWTA2 as
        HCWTA1∪HCWTA2
     }
   Unlock the corresponding items of HCWTT in the OSS;
end procedure
```

When a VM is closed, our design needs to determine whether the VM is the last one in the node. According to the requirement of covert flows confinement, the nodes cannot run VMs belonging to different coalitions at the same time. So in a moment a node can only belong to a coalition, or has not been occupied by any coalition. Therefore, if there is no VM running in the node, this node can be released to join the new coalition in the next time. The above can be described as follows: when a VM in a node is closed, the LSS of the node will check whether the VM is the last one in the node. If it is not, the LSS just closes the VM and does not change HCWTA of the node. Otherwise, the LSS closes the VM and empties its HCWTA, while informing the OSS to update HCWTT. The OSS will check whether there is another node which belongs to this coalition, if not, the OSS will empty the HCWTA-related item of HCWTT.

When we enforce the above covert flows confinement mechanism in the VM-based cloud computing environment, VMs within the same coalition are allowed for communication through an open channel and covert channel, and VMs in different coalitions are prohibited to exchange with any information flows.

4   CFCC Evaluation

4.1   Implementation of CFCC

To verify our covert flows confinement mechanism, we implement a prototype which exploits the existing policy enforcement modules of sHype based on Xen 3.1.0. The prototype system consists of 4 machines connected with a 1000Mbit Ethernet. Three nodes used as LSSes is a 2.33 GHz Intel Core Duo processor with 2 MB L2 cache, 2 GB RAM and an 80 GB 7200 RPM disk. The OSS is Pentium 4 machine with 2GHz, 2GB RAM and Federal Linux installed.

The OSS is implemented as two parts: one is a Policy Management Module (PMM) which is a stand-alone daemon running in Federal Linux, handling the requirements of synchronization between each LSS and the OSS; the other is a policy database acting as a policy center to store all HCWTAs from each LSS.

As mainly used for policy enforcement, the LSS is relatively complicated, and it consists of three main modules: Local Policy Management Module (LPMM), Policy Cache Module (PCM) and Policy Enforcement Module (PEM). In our design, the PCM caches the local system state information and requires policies related to local node. The LPMM is responsible for communicating with the PMM of the OSS and keeps synchronization between the PCM in the LSS and the policy database in the OSS through the secure network communication channels.

The PEM is divided into two parts: one is located in Dom0, which is responsible for controlling the migration and communication of VMs between nodes and the other is the Access Control Module (ACM) of sHype [1], located in Xen hypervisor. The PEM in Dom0, named Inter-node Access Control Module, enforces policies by inserting specific hooks into the existing communication and migration modules. That is, executing hooks in virtual bridge can control the communication of inter-node VMs and inspect all network packets from and to the node. A Communication and Control Module (CMCM) is established to control the network access according to the PCM.

The ACM of sHype is used to control the VM start in local node. We exploit the existing control mechanism of sHype to simplify out implementation. The ACM makes the decision whether a labeled VM is allowed to start or not through the *conflict_aggregate_set* and *running_types* array. The *running_types* array stores the labels of VMs which are running in the node, and the *conflict_aggregate_set* array records the labels which are in conflict with the labels of VMs running in the node. We propose an algorithm of VM start by modifying the functions of the ACM, including *chwall_domain_destroy*, *chwall_pre_domain_create*, and *chwall_post_domain_create*.

The OSS and LSS are both written in C. More complex policies and hooks can be added to extend our prototype, which makes such changes relatively simple. In addition, our implementation doesn't make any changes on the OS kernel of Dom0.

4.2 Effectiveness Analysis

We conduct an experiment with our prototype system to analyze the effectiveness of CFCC. There are four kinds of VM labels, including Oil-A, Oil-B, Bank-C and Other. The labels are named after the workload of different companies, and conflicts of interest exist between company Oil-A and Oil-B. So the conflict set is {(Oil-A, Oil-B)}, which implies that any flows between VMs with conflicts of interest are prohibited.

The security policy is written in XML and stored in the OSS. In the initial stage, each node respectively runs VMs with different labels. We can see that our mechanism can confine the direct covert flows and transitive covert flows when VMs start, migration and communication happen.

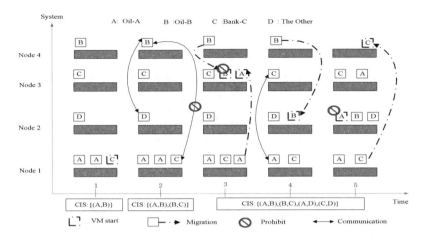

Fig. 2. A scenario of covert flows confinement

As shown in figure 2, in moment 1, when Back-C[2] tries to start in node 1, we note the CIS as {(Oil-A, Oil-B)}. So we can risk the covert flows leakage between Bank-C and Oil-A, and Bank-C is permitted to start in node 1. Then Bank-C and Oil-A consti-tute a new coalition, and they have the same conflict of interest relationship. In moment 2, when Bank-B wants to communicate with Bank-C and other, Bank-C and Oil-A in the same coalition and the conflict of interest set has become {(Oil-A, Oil-B), (Oil-B, Bank-C)}. So the requirement of communication between Oil-B and Bank-C will be denied. But Oil-B and other has no conflict of interest, the require-ment of communication between them is permitted, and they will constitute a new coalition. Finally there are two coalitions {Oil-A, Bank-C} and {Oil-B, other}. The coalitions are built dynamically according to the conflict set, and VM start, communi-cation or migration sequence.

In moment 3 and 4, communications between VMs and migration of VMs within the same coalition are permitted and those between different coalitions are denied. In moment 5, the nodes cannot run VMs belonging to different coalitions because in a moment a node can only belong to a coalition. But when there are no VMs running in the node, this node is released from a coalition and can join another coalition.

4.3 Performance Analysis

As shown in Figure 3, by compared with normal or sHype-enforced VM start process, our prototype has a marked increase (about 15% to normal) in overhead of perform-ance when VMs start in single-node environment. The increasing overhead are mainly caused by not only the modification of the added dynamic HCWTA (*con-flict_aggregate_set* and *running_types* array), but also the replication of dynamic PCW policy information from Xen VMM to the PCM. Since the access control hooks in local nodes are invoked only by domain operations, and a 15% increase in per-formance overhead is acceptable.

---

[2] We just simply use a label to represent a VM with the label.

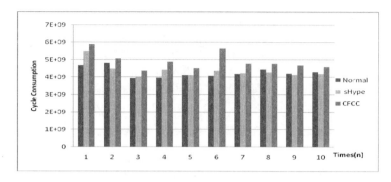

Fig. 3. Overhead in VMs start (single-node)

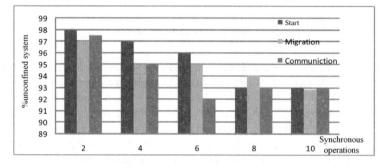

Fig. 4. Synchronization overhead

The performance overhead is mainly caused by the synchronization between the OSS and any LSS. When a new VM starts, the VM try to communicate with another VM in another node or a VM want to be migrated to another node, the centralized information exchange need lock the related items of HCWTT in the OSS. When the other LSSes need access the locked items, they must wait until the items are un-locked. In figure 4, we can see that the overhead of synchronization increases with the number of concurrent operations, but the increasing overhead is acceptable because in our system, each local node buffers the state of the coalitions and most decisions can be made in local nodes. Only when new labels which do not belong to the coalition are required, the local node needs to communicate with the OSS. As for an application, because the number of labels is limited, so the growth of synchroniza-tion overhead has a maximum and is acceptable.

5   Conclusions and Future Work

Trusted Virtual coalition (domain)[5][7][8][15] can be used to manage resources and control information flows in VM-based cloud computing environment. Because VMM is an Infrastructure of cloud computing, it is natural that resources are allocated in VM granularity. Our contribution in this paper aims to provide a mechanism to confine the covert flows (CFCC) which become a problem for VM-based cloud computing environments even enforced with mandatory access control (MAC). The proposed mechanism satisfies the enterprise level security requirement to assure that valuable information on such systems would not be leaked to the competitors, but can permit information leakage by the covert channels between different departments of the same company. Experimental results show that the performance overhead is acceptable. In our future work, we plan to add application level information flows control for virtual machine coalitions.

References

1. Buyya, R., Yeo, C.S., Venugopal, S.: Market-oriented Cloud Computing: Vision, Hype, and Reality for Delivering IT Services as Computing Utilities. In: 10th IEEE Conference on High Performance Computing and Communications, pp. 5–13. IEEE Press, Dalian (2008)
2. Armbrust, M., Fox, A., Griffith, R., Joseph, A.D., Katz, R., Konwinski, A., Lee, G., Patterson, D., Rabkin, A., Stoica, I., Zaharia, M.: Above the Clouds: A Berkeley View of Cloud Computing. Technical Report, EECS, University of California at Berkeley (2009)
3. Berger, S., Caceres, R., Pendarakis, D., Sailer, R., Valdez, E., Perez, R., Schildhauer, W., Srinivasan, D.: TVDc: Managing Security in the Trusted Virtual Datacenter. ACM SIGOPS Operating Systems Review 42, 40–47 (2008)
4. Sailer, R., Jaeger, T., Valdez, E., Caceres, R., Perez, R., Berger, S., Griffin, J.L., Doorn, L.V.: Building a MAC-Based Security Architecture for the Xen Open-source Hypervisor. In: 21st Annual Computer Security Applications Conference, pp. 276–285. IEEE Press, Tucson (2005)
5. Commercial Technology in High Assurance Applications, http://www.vmware.com/pdf/TechTrendNotes.pdf
6. McCune, J.M., Jaeger, T., Berger, S., Caceres, R., Sailer, R.: Shamon: A System for Distributed Mandatory Access Control. In: 22nd Annual Computer Security Applications Conference, pp. 23–32. IEEE Press, Miami Beach (2006)
7. Griffin, J.L., Jaeger, T., Perez, R., Sailer, R., Doorn, L.V., Caceres, R.: Trusted Virtual Domains: Toward Secure Distributed Services. In: 1st IEEE Workshop on Hot Topics in System Dependability, Yokohama (2005)
8. Cabuk, S., Dalton, C.I., Ramasamy, H., Schunter, M.: Towards Automated Provisioning of Secure Virtualized Networks. In: 14th ACM conference on Computer and communications security, pp. 235–245. ACM, Alexandria (2007)
9. Proctor, N.E., Neumann, P.G.: Architectural Implications of Covert Channels. In: 15th National Computer Security Conference, Baltimore, pp. 28–43 (1992)
10. Jaeger, T., Edwards, A., Zhang, X.: Consistency Analysis of Authorization Hook Placement in the Linux Security Modules Framework. ACM Transactions on Information and System Security 7, 175–205 (2004)
11. Zhang, X., Edwards, A., Jaeger, T.: Using CQUAL for Static Analysis of Authorization Hook Placement. In: 11th USENIX Security Symposium, pp. 33–48. USENIX, San Francisco (2002)
12. Cheng, G., Jin, H., Zhou, D., Ohoussou, A.K., Zhao, F.: A Prioritized Chinese Wall Model for Managing the Covert Information Flows in Virtual Machine Systems. In: 9th International Conference for Young Computer Scientists, pp. 1481–1487. IEEE Press, Hunan (2008)

13. Jaeger, T., Sailer, R., Sreenivasan, Y.: Managing the Risk of Covert Information Flows in Virtual Machine Systems. In: 12th ACM symposium on Access control Models and Technologies, pp. 81–90. ACM, Sophia Antipolis (2007)
14. Boeboert, W.E., Kain, R.Y.: A Practical Alternative to Hierarchical Integrity Policies. In: 8th National Computer Security Conference, Gaithersburg (1985)
15. Sadeghi, A.R., Stuble, C.: Towards Multilateral-Secure DRM Platforms. In: Deng, R.H., Bao, F., Pang, H., Zhou, J. (eds.) ISPEC 2005. LNCS, vol. 3439, pp. 326–337. Springer, Heidelberg (2005)
16. Trusted Computing Group, https://www.trustedcomputinggroup.org
17. Berger, S., Cáceres, R., Goldman, K., Perez, R., Sailer, R., Doorn, L.V.: vTPM: Virtualizing the Trusted Platform Module. In: 15th USENIX Security Symposium, Vancouver (2006)
18. Jaeger, T., Sailer, R., Shankar, U.: PRIMA: Policy-Reduced Integrity Measurement Architecture. In: 11th ACM Symposium on Access Control Models and Technologies, pp. 19–28. ACM, Lake Tahoe (2006)
19. Sailer, R., Zhang, X., Jaeger, T., Doorn, L.V.: Design and Implementation of a TCG-based Integrity Measurement Architecture. In: 13th conference on USENIX Security Symposium, pp. 16–31. USENIX, San Diego (2004)
20. Valdez, E., Sailer, R., Perez, R.: Retrofitting the IBM POWER Hypervisor to Support Mandatory Access Control. In: 23rd Annual Computer Security Applications Conference, pp. 221–231. IEEE Press, Miami Beach (2007)
21. Barham, P., Dragovic, B., Fraser, K., Hand, S., Harris, T., Ho, A., Neugebauer, R., Pratt, I., Warfield, A.: Xen and the Art of Virtualization. In: 19th ACM symposium on Operating systems principles, pp. 164–177. ACM, Bolton Landing (2003)
22. Schellhorn, G., Reif, W., Schairer, A., Karger, P., Austel, V., Toll, D.: Verification of a Formal Security Model for Multiapplicative Smart Cards. In: Cuppens, F., Deswarte, Y., Gollmann, D., Waidner, M. (eds.) ESORICS 2000. LNCS, vol. 1895, pp. 17–36. Springer, Heidelberg (2000)
23. Brewer, D.F.C., Nash, M.J.: The Chinese Wall Security Policy. In: 1989 IEEE Symposium on Security and Privacy, pp. 206–214. IEEE Press, Oakland (1989)

Automatic Cache Update Control for Scalable Resource Information Service with WS-Management

Kumiko Tadano, Fumio Machida, Masahiro Kawato, and Yoshiharu Maeno

Service Platforms Research Laboratories, NEC Corporation, Kawasaki, Japan
{k-tadano@bq,h-machida@ab,m-kawato@ap,y-maeno@aj}jp.nec.com

Abstract. Scalable and interoperable security management has become an important issue in advanced datacenter services. In our previous work, we had developed integrated access control manager (IAM) that manages accesses to various resources. To integrate access controls for various resources, a scalable and interoperable resource information service that provides target resource information to compose access control policies is required. To improve interoperability and performance of the resource information service, we brought a resource information cache into the IAM and introduced an automatic cache update control method that updates cached information proactively based on WS-Management and CIM standards. To reduce server loads to update cached information, the proposed method selects a part of cached information by content priority as an update target instead of updating all cached contents. We evaluated the average query response time of resource information service by simulating the proposed method. The proposed method reduced average query response time by 66.66% compared to the conventional reactive update control method.

Keywords: Caching, prefetching, resource information service, web service.

1 Introduction

Scalable and interoperable security management has become an important issue in advanced datacenter services that host many enterprise applications. Many companies still have concerns for security and reliability of consolidate server systems using virtualization due to the risk of spreading of security incidents or performance problems across the systems. Consolidated security management is a crucial but complex task for system administrators, because they have to configure all the security modules for a large number of managed resources properly and consistently.

The Secure Platform project (SPF) tackles this issue by developing access control management middleware with secure components for operating systems and virtualization software based on the standards. The middleware provides a common interface to compose security policies in order to control access to various resources such as virtual machines, operating systems, and applications on many managed hosts. The middleware automatically transforms the composed policies into concrete policies for individual resources using information schemas of various resources.

L. Boursas et al. (Eds.): SVM 2009, CCIS 71, pp. 55–66, 2010.

The middleware is designed with the Common Information Model [4] and the WS-Management protocol [9] to promote interoperability with third party software.

To compose access control policies for target systems, a large amount of information on various resources is required. It takes long time to collect resource information from lots of remote managed hosts on demand. An effective way to improve the performance of the resource information service is to introduce a resource information cache that stores retrieved resource information temporarily into the management server. However, the cached information may not be up-to-date since resource information is originally variable. To keep cached resource information up-to-date, cache update control for the resource information cache is required.

Conventional cache update control methods for resource information cache cannot scale under the restriction of the freshness of cached resource information and the limited server capacity. A simple approach to update resource information cache is the notification-based cache update: an agent in a managed host notifies resource state changes to the manager. In this method, there is a possibility to get too many notifications from many agents at a time, which causes the "flash crowd" [1]. The other approach is to update cached information reactively when cache miss occurs. The cache mechanism for a web proxy is a typical example of the reactive approach. CERN httpd [12], DeleGate [13] the Harvest Cache Daemon [15] and its successor Squid [14] are well known web proxy caches. In the reactive update method such as proxy caches, once cached information expires, it will not be updated unless anyone accesses it again. It always takes long time to retrieve resource information for the first time after expiration. An effective way to avoid the drawback of the reactive method is to update cached information proactively and periodically. As a proactive cache update control method, an algorithm to schedule cache-update processes is proposed in Ref. [2]. By scheduling updates, the proposed algorithm updates whole resource information in the cache with a stable load. However, the algorithm cannot be applied to large-scale systems, since the algorithm updates whole resource information and needs to run too many update processes.

In this paper, we propose an automatic cache update control method for resource information cache that can apply to large scale systems based on the proactive method. The proposed method updates only a part of resource information in the cache selectively based on some criteria to predict query request rate, instead of updating whole resource information.

The rest of this paper is organized as follows. In Section 2, outline of Secure Platform is introduced. In Section 3, we propose the cache update control method for the resource information cache. Experimental evaluation of query performance of the middleware is presented in Section 4. Simulation evaluation of the proposed method using the results obtained in Section 4 is described in Section 5. In Section 6, related studies are explained. Finally Section 7 provides the conclusions and future directions.

2 Secure Platform

To integrate access controls for various resources, the SPF project provides an architecture of the integrated access control manager (IAM) [12].

The IAM provides a graphical user interface to compose access control policies in a uniform way and a function to automatically convert the composed policies to concrete policies for individual access control module, and distributes the converted policies to individual access control module (see Fig. 1). The privileged OS in Fig. 1 is a special OS that manages virtualization platform. For example, Xen's hypervisor is managed by a privileged OS called dom0. The IAM employs Common Information Model (CIM) standards [4] which provide a common definition of management information for various resources in order to manage several access control modules for different resources uniformly. To facilitate communication with third party tools, the communication protocol between the IAM and its agents on the managed hosts is based on the WS-Management standard [9] which is the SOAP-based protocol for management of various resources. The IAM requires lots of resource information to compose the access control policies and to convert the composed policies to concrete policies for specific resources at the policy distribution.

Resource Information Manager is a component of the IAM that collects and manages information of various resources in the common manner based on the CIM and the WS-Management standards. The Resource Information Manager receives queries from clients and provides the requested resource information to the clients. The Resource Information Manager has a resource information cache to improve the query performance. If the requested information is in the cache (*cache hit*), Resource Information Manager provides the cached information to the client. If the requested information is not in the cache or the cached information is invalid (*cache miss*), the Resource Information Manager retrieves the requested information from a remote managed host, stores it in the cache and provides it to the client.

The cache hit rate of the resource information cache affects directly to the performance of the IAM. If cache misses occur frequently, the Resource Information Manager may require considerable time to provide the requested resource information since it takes long time to retrieve resource information from remote hosts. Due to the long delays of the resource information queries, the performance of the policy composing and policy translating by the IAM degrades especially in the large scale systems.

To improve cache hit rate, this paper introduces a proactive cache update method for resource information cache into the Resource Information Manager. We describe an architecture of the proactive cache update control method for large-scale system in the next section.

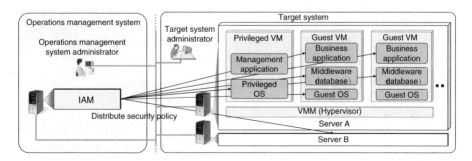

Fig. 1. Architecture of Secure Platform project

3   Resource Information Cache Update Control

We propose an automatic cache update control method to improve the hit rate for resource information cache.

3.1   Architecture

The Resource Information Manager consists of four components: *resource informa-tion cache*, *resource information cache update controller*, *query processor*, and *resource information collector* as shown in Figure 2. The query processor receives a query for resource information from the policy manager of the IAM, and provides requested resource information to the policy manager. As a query language for CIM, the IAM employs CIM Query Language (CQL) [11] which is a subset of Structured Query Language (SQL) with some extensions specific to the CIM. The query proces-sor provides the cached information to the policy manager if requested information is in the cache and valid. Otherwise the query processor provides the requested informa-tion retrieved by the resource information collector. The resource information collec-tor retrieves requested resource information from an agent in a remote managed host based on the WS-Management protocol. The protocol handler in the agent receives the WS-Management based request from the resource information collector, returns the requested resource information retrieved through the CIM Object Manager (CI-MOM). The CIMOM provides information of system resources using providers complying with Common Manageability Programming Interface (CMPI) [20]. Re-source information cache update controller (CUC) periodically selects the cached resource information to update it. Then the CUC sends requests to collect recent data of the selected resource information from the remote hosts, receives the responses, and updates resource information in the cache. The CUC may improve the cache hit rate of the resource information cache by selecting the cached information most likely to be queried as an update target. The selection method of update targets is an essen-tial part of the CUC to improve the cache hit rate.

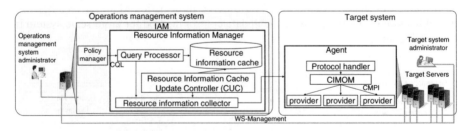

Fig. 2. Architecture of Resource Information Manager

3.2   Update Target Selection Process

The proposed resource information cache update controller works under the following conditions:

(i)   The number of resources whose information is updated during a certain time interval $t_{interval}$ is limited by m.

(ii) Cached Information of each resource has expiration time that is denoted as time to live (*TTL*).

A piece of information of a resource corresponds to an instance of a CIM class representing a resource such as a host, a filesystem, a service, etc. As the number of resources whose information is updated per unit time increases, server loads to update resource information also increases. Therefore condition (i) is required to avoid making the IAM server overload due to the too many update processes. The value of m is smaller than the total number of resources $|R|$. By condition (ii), if a resource r_i ($i = 1, 2,...|R|$) has time to live TTL_i, cached information of r_i expires when it has been stored longer than TTL_i without being updated. If time to expiration of r_i is shorter than the length of time T_{ex}, r_i becomes a candidate for update.

The proposed CUC works as follows:

(1) Select resources whose cached information will expire within T_{ex} as candidates for update.

(2) Select update targets in order of priority (discussed later) from the candidates selected in step (1).

(3) Collect the selected resource information though the resource information collector.

(4) Update information in the cache with collected resource information.

(5) Repeat step (1) to step (4) at a certain update interval $t_{interval}$.

In step (2), some criteria of selecting update targets are required. Typical examples of criteria are frequency of references, total number of references, the last access time and data sizes. The Resource Information Manager employs several criteria to predict system administrator's access patterns based on the history of access logs. However, the accuracy of the employed prediction algorithms is not discussed in this paper.

The proposed cache controller improves scalability of resource information management. The CUC updates only a part of cached resource information instead of updating all resource information as shown in the conventional approach [2]. By selecting a part of resources from lots of managed resources as update targets, the CUC can improve cache hit rate in the large-scale systems. Query response time depends on selecting method of resource information to be updated in the cache. Query response time with different update control methods is evaluated in Section 5.

4 Experiments

In this section, we describe the results of basic performance evaluation of the implemented IAM and Resource Information Manager.

4.1 Experimental Setup

We implemented the IAM in the previous work [7]. We incorporated the proposed CUC into the Resource Information Manager of the IAM. The resource information cache is implemented with MySQL. The MySQL database stores resource information and its expiration time. As a protocol handler for WS-Management, Openwsman [21] is used. The agent in the managed host is implemented with Openwsman and Small-Footprint CIM Broker [17].

For evaluating the performance of the Resource Information Manager, we set up a testing environment shown in Fig. 3. The management server and the target server are connected to each other. The Resource Information Manager and a client are installed on the management server. The Resource Information Manager retrieves resource information from an agent installed on the target server.

The query performance is measured by the query response time of CQLs requested by a client in the management server. Each CQL requests to retrieve an instance of CIM class such as CIM_ComputerSystem, CIM_EnabledLogicalElementCapabilities, CIM_FileSystem, CIM_LogicalFile, and SPF_Directory (see [7]). If the requested instance is cached in the database, then the Resource Information Manager checks the expiration time of the instance. If the instance is unexpired, this situation is regarded as a *cache hit* and the Resource Information Manager provides the cached instance to the client. If the requested instance is expired or not in the database, a *cache miss* occurs and the Resource Information Manager retrieves the instance from the agent in the remote host based on the WS-Management protocol and stores it in the database.

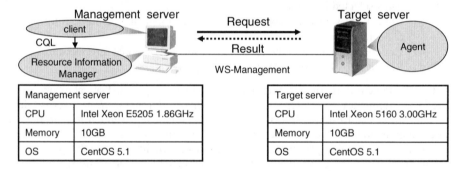

Fig. 3. Configuration of the test bed for response time measurements

Table 1. Response time and the size of the response message of each query for Resource Information Manager

Query target	CQL	Response time [sec]		Size of response message [bytes]
		Cache miss	Cache hit	
CIM_ComputerSystem	SELECT * FROM CIM_ComputerSystem WHERE Name='hostA'	3.0691	0.0043	1734
CIM_FileSystem	SELECT * FROM CIM_FileSystem WHERE Name='/'	1.0686	0.0042	1886
SPF_Directory	SELECT * FROM SPF_Directory WHERE Name='/etc/'	0.0705	0.0046	8979
CIM_LogicalFile	SELECT * FROM CIM_LogicalFile WHERE Name='/etc/yum.conf'	0.0411	0.0053	1496
CIM_EnabledLogicalElementCapabilities	SELECT * FROM CIM_EnabledLogicalElementCapabilities	1.0939	0.0044	1557
Average		1.0686	0.0046	3130

4.2 Results

The results of average query response time of each CQL and the size of corresponding response message are shown in Table 1. The response time of each CQL was measured in the cases of both cache hit and cache miss. Each experiment was repeated 10 times and the average query response times are calculated.

Average values of query response time in the cases of cache miss and cache hit are 1.0686 seconds and 0.0046 seconds, respectively. We used these values in the simulation of the CUC described in Section 5.

5 Simulation Studies

To evaluate the CUC in a consistent and systematic manner, we simulate the CUC in the maximally effective case and in the minimally effective case: the CUC updates the resources with high query request rates optimally and the CUC updates resources just randomly regardless of their query request rates. Using the results of experimental evaluation shown in Section 4, we present simulation of three different update control methods for comparison: optimum and random proactive update control methods of the CUC and the conventional reactive method.

5.1 Simulation of the CUC

We evaluate query response time in three different ways of update control for resource information cache by simulation using the results obtained from the measurements in Section 4. The purpose of performing a simulation is to understand the effect of the proposed cache update control method. We do not evaluate the CUC in the real enterprise systems in this paper. Instead, we evaluate the CUC by simulation using the measurements obtained in Section 4 as preliminary steps for the evaluation in real environment. We focus on Resource Information Manager only. We assume that the Resource Information Manager receives query requests in a constant query request rate s_i for each target resource r_i.

Following three update control methods are evaluated for comparison.

- *Op-proactive*: *Optimal proactive update*
  Op-proactive method selects update target resources whose cached information will expire within T_{ex} in descending order of query request rate.
- *Rd-proactive*: *Random proactive update*
  Rd-proactive method selects update target resources whose cached information will expire within T_{ex} randomly and update them proactively.
- *Reactive*: *Reactive update*
  Reactive method updates resource information only when cache miss occurs. Web proxy server uses this method to update cached information.

Op-proactive method corresponds to the update control of the CUC in the maximally effective case where the query request rate of each resource can be completely estimated by the prediction method as shown in Section 3.2. On the other hand, rd-proactive method corresponds to the update control of the CUC in the minimally effective case where query request rate of each resource is not predictable by the prediction method at all, as a consequence, the CUC just randomly updates information of resources which will expire in the near future.

5.2 Simulation Procedure

Simulation parameters are given as follows. Let the average query response time in case of cache hit be T_{hit}, meanwhile let the average query response time in case of cache miss be T_{miss}. Obviously T_{hit} is larger than T_{miss}. We define s_i as steady-state query request rate of a resource r_i. We define t_{start} as start time of simulation, t_{end} as ending time.

The parameters are configured as follows. s_i and time to live TTL_i are uniform pseudorandom numbers in the range of 0 to 1 and 0 [sec] to 10 [sec], respectively. We assume TTL_i is constant throughout the simulation and TTL_i does not correlate with s_i. Note that the correlation of s_i and TTL_i affects cache hit ratio. For example, if information of a resource tends to have long time to live and high query request rate, resource information that hardly expires is often queried. Above trend is persistent because we assume that TTL_i and s_i is constant throughout the simulation as we mentioned before. In order to make TTL_i and s_i uncorrelated, we generated random numbers for arrays of TTL and s by Mersenne Twister Method [5] with different random seeds. The correlation coefficient between two arrays is less than 0.01. We set t_{start} to 0 and t_{end} to 200 [sec]. The value of the update interval $t_{interval}$ is set to 5 [sec]. Average query response time T_{res} is calculated according to the following equation:

$$T_{res} = p\, T_{hit} + (\,1 - p\,)\, T_{miss}. \tag{1}$$

where p is cache hit rate obtained from simulation.

The simulation is performed according to the following steps:

Step 1. Extract cached resource information whose remaining time before expiration is less than T_{ex}.

Step 2. Select resources whose information is updated from the extracted resource information in step 1 up to m.

Step 3. Update expiration time of resource information selected in step 2 with the summation of the current time and TTL_i.

Step 4. Obtain the cache hit rate p by simulating query requests with the query request rate s_i and calculate T_{res} from the equation (1).

Step 5. Repeat step 1 to step 4 from t_{start} to t_{end} at a certain update interval $t_{interval}$.

In case of the reactive method, steps 1-3 are skipped. Instead, the reactive method updates expiration time of resource information which is queried in step 4 with the summation of the current time and TTL_i.

5.3 Simulation Results

5.3.1 Effects of Varying T_{ex} on T_{res}

We evaluate the hit rate p and the average query response time T_{res} by varying the threshold of time to live T_{ex} in the range of -10 [sec] to 10 [sec]. T_{hit} is set to 0.0046 [sec], T_{miss} is set to 1.0686 [sec] based on the actual measurements in Section 4. Fig. 4

shows the results of p and T_{res} plotted against T_{ex}. In case of the op-proactive method, the minimum value of T_{res} is 0.219 [sec] per query at $T_{ex} = 0$. T_{res} obtained by op-proactive method is reduced by 0.850 [sec] (79.52%) at $T_{ex} = 0$ from the value of T_{miss}. In case of the rd-proactive method, the minimum value of T_{res} is 0.451 seconds at $T_{ex} = -1$. T_{res} obtained by rd-proactive method is reduced by 0.618 [sec] (57.83%) at $T_{ex} = -1$ from the value of T_{miss}.

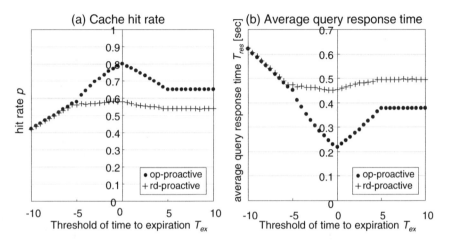

Fig. 4. Results of the hit rate and the average query response time against the threshold of time to expiration

5.3.2 Effects of Varying m on T_{res}

We evaluate the hit rate p and the average query response time T_{res} by varying the number of resources whose information is updated per update interval m in the range of 0 to 1000. T_{hit} and T_{miss} are set to the same values in 5.3.1. Figure 5 shows the results of p and T_{res} plotted against m. T_{ex} is set to 0 [sec] as the optimum value for the op-proactive method obtained in 5.3.1, and set to 10 [sec] as the worst value because it is larger than any TTL_i and all resource become candidates for update.

We investigate the variation of T_{res} due to the difference of threshold of time to expiration T_{ex} in the same update control method. By proper adjustment of T_{ex}, T_{res} is reduced by 0.083 [sec] (23.55%) averagely, and 0.159 [sec] (39.52%) at the maximum at $m=380$ per query in the op-proactive method.

We evaluate the performance of the CUC depending on the selection method of update target resource information by comparing the op-proactive method with the rd-proactive method. T_{res} of op-proactive method is reduced by 0.111 [sec] (29.34%) averagely at $T_{ex} = 0$, and 0.237 [sec] (49.39%) at the maximum at $m=380$ and $T_{ex}=0$ per query compared to that of rd-proactive method.

We evaluate the performance improvements by the introduction of proposed op-proactive method in comparison with conventional reactive method. T_{res} of op-proactive method is reduced by 0.536 [sec](66.66%) averagely, and 0.738 [sec] (98.31%) at the maximum at $m=840$ per query compared to that of the reactive method.

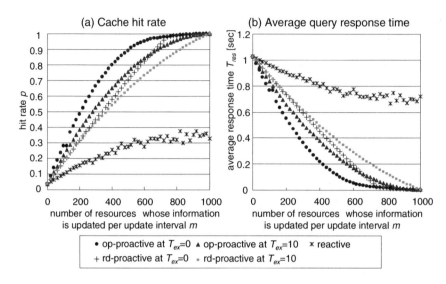

Fig. 5. Results of the hit rate (a) and the average query response time (b) against the number of resources whose information is updated per update interval

In this paper, average query response time is evaluated by simulation experiment of the CUC based on the measurements of query performance of the IAM in the laboratory environment. We assumed that the query request rate is given in this simulation. However, in real environment, we need to estimate the query request rate by the degree of reference such as frequency of references, total number of references, last access time and so on.

6 Related Work

To improve the cache hit rate and reduce latency in accessing data, there are several techniques related to the cache control and prefetching of Web contents [16][3]. Teng et al. [22] propose a cache replacement algorithm, which considers both the caching effect in the Web environment and the prefetching rules provided by various prefetching schemes. Their proposed algorithm replaces cached information in an event driven way, so the load to retrieve information is not evenly balanced in contrast to the periodically scheduled update control method presented in this paper.

There are some useful methods associated with access control in large-scale, heterogeneous systems. For access control in a dynamic distributed environment, it is beneficial to consider multiple resources as a single abstract resource because it simplifies defining policies. An approach to produce low level concrete policies from the high level abstract policy automatically by considering resources as a single abstract hierarchical resource is presented in Ref. [6]. Unlike the CUC in this paper, the proposed method in Ref. [6] has no mechanism to collect resource information necessary for converting abstract policies to concrete policies for individual resources in a short time. For management interoperability among multi-vendor systems, Common Information Model (CIM) [4] standards are widely-used. We have proposed an extension of CIM Schema for improving the performance of directory search in previous work [7]. Along with Small Footprint CIM Broker [17] used in this paper, OpenPegasus [18] is also well known as a CIM Object Manager. Preliminary performance evaluation of Small Footprint CIM Broker and OpenPegasus is shown in Ref. [19]. The response time of Small Footprint CIM Broker is shorter than that of OpenPegasus. On the other hand, there are some standards of web service for interoperability: WSDM [8] and WS-Management [9]. Performance evaluation of these two standards is shown in Ref. [10].

7 Conclusion

In this paper, we proposed an automatic cache update control method for the resource information service based on the WS-Management and the CIM standards to reduce average query response time in large-scale systems. To reduce the load of the IAM server to update cached resource information, the proposed method selects a part of resource information to update it from all cached resource information. The proposed method improves cache hit rate under the limited server capacity. We evaluated cache hit rate and average query response time by simulating three different update control methods with given query request rate s_i and the results of experimental evaluation. The proposed method reduces the average query response time by 0.536 seconds (66.66%) averagely, and 0.738 seconds (98.31%) at the maximum per query in optimum case compared to that of conventional reactive update control method.

A further direction of this study will be to evaluate the proposed method in the real enterprise systems. In this paper we assumed the query request rate to be given accurately in the simulation. However, in real environment, the query request rate is predicted based on the system administrator's previous access patterns for update target selection by the proposed method. The query response time depends on the accuracy of the prediction. The comparative evaluation of the query response time obtained from both the simulation and the experiment in the enterprise systems will be discussed in a future paper.

Acknowledgments

This work is a part of Secure Platform project supported by Japanese Ministry of Economy, Trade and Industry, and Association of Super-Advanced Electronics Technologies.

References

1. Desai, R., Tilak, S., Gandhi, B., Lewis, M.J., Abu-Ghazaleh, N.B.: Analysis of Query Maching Criteria and Resource Monitoring Models for Grid Application Scheduling. In: 6th IEEE International Symposium on Cluster Computing and the Grid, CCGrid 2006 (2006)
2. Machida, F., Kawato, M., Maeno, Y.: Guarantee of Freshness in Resource Information Cache on WSPE: Web Service Polling Engine. In: CCGrid 2006 (2006)

3. Lempel, R., Moran, S.: Optimizing Result Prefetching in Web Search Engines with Segmented Indices. ACM Trans. Internet Technology 4(1), 31–59 (2004)
4. Common Information Model (CIM) Standards,
   http://www.dmtf.org/standards/cim/
5. Matsumoto, M., Nishimura, T.: Mersenne twister: A 623-dimensionally equidistributed uniform pseudorandom number generator. ACM Trans. on Modeling and Computer Simulations (1998)
6. Su, L., Chadwick, D.W., Basden, A., Cunningham, J.A.: Automated Decomposition of Access Control Policies. In: Proceedings of the Sixth IEEE International Workshop on Policies for Distributed Systems and Networks (2005)
7. Machida, F., Tadano, K., Kawato, M., Ishikawa, T., Morita, Y., Nakae, M.: CIM-based Resource Information Management for Integrated Access Control Manager. In: SVM 2008 (2008)
8. WSDM/MUWS,   http://docs.oasis-open.org/wsdm/wsdm-muws1-1.1-spec-os-01.pdf
9. WS-Management,
   http://www.dmtf.org/standards/published_documents/DSP0226_1.0.0.pdf
10. Moreira, G.M., Silvestrin, G., Sanchez, R.N., Gaspary, L.P.: On the Performance of Web Services Management Standards for Network Management - An Evaluation of MUWS and WS-Management. In: Proc. of the IFIP/IEEE Int. Symp. on Integrated Network Management (IM 2007), pp. 459–468 (2007)
11. CIM Query Language Specification (DSP0202), http://www.dmtf.org/standards/published_documents/DSP0202.pdf
12. CERN httpd, http://www.w3.org/Daemon/
13. DeleGate, http://www.delegate.org/delegate/
14. Squid, http://www.squid-cache.org
15. Chankhunthod, A., Danzig, P., Neerdaels, C., Schwartz, M., Worrell, K.: A hierarchical internet object cache. In: Proc. of the 1996 USENIX Technical Conf., pp. 153–163 (1996)
16. Yang, Q., Zhang, H.H.: Integrating Web Prefetching and Caching Using Prediction Models. World Wide Web 4(4), 299–321 (2001)
17. Small Footprint CIM Broker (SFCB),
   http://sblim.wiki.sourceforge.net/Sfcb
18. OpenPegasus, http://www.openpegasus.org/
19. Schuur, A.: sfcb Small Footprint Cim Broker Introduction,
   http://sblim.wiki.sourceforge.net/space/showimage/sfcb-intro-ext.pdf
20. Systems Management: Common Manageability Programming Interface (CMPI),
   http://www.opengroup.org/pubs/catalog/c051.htm
21. Openwsman, http://www.openwsman.org/
22. Teng, W.-G., Chang, C.-Y., Chen, M.-S.: IEEE Transactions on Parallel and Distributed Systems 16(5), 444–455 (May 2005)

Fast Booting Many Similar Virtual Machines

Xiaolin Wang[1], Zhenlin Wang[2], Shuang Liang[1], Zhengyi Zhang[1],
Yingwei Luo[1], and Xiaoming Li[1]

[1] Dept. of Computer Science and Technology, Peking University, Beijing, China, 100871
[2] Dept. of Computer Science, Michigan Technological University, USA
{wxl,lyw,lxm}@pku.edu.cn, zlwang@mtu.edu

Abstract. Virtual Machines have been commonly used for server consolidation in data centers, network classrooms, and cloud computing environments. Although booting up a virtual machine takes much less time than booting up a physical computer, booting up multiple virtual machines on a single physical server still takes a lot of time. We propose a method to speed up the booting process when a set of similar virtual machines share a snapshot enabled storage. Our method exploits massive memory page sharing stemming from the reads to common disk blocks by these virtual machines. Our experiments show that the second virtual machine may reduce the booting time by half.

1 Introduction

Virtualization has become a backbone technique in data centers supporting cloud computing [1][2][3]. Since a virtual machine runs on the virtualized hardware, normally, booting up a virtual machine takes quite less time than booting up a physical computer, since, during the booting process, a physical computer usually needs to initialize all the hardware devices and wait for their response.

In many situations, the software stack of all virtual machines is quite similar to each other. Figure 1 shows a network classroom application, each terminal connects to a virtual machine, and their operation systems are the same and configurations are similar; they run the same set of applications; and they serve the same kind of users.

To speedup the booting process of those similar virtual machines, one effective way is to setup a base virtual machine on the snapshot-enabled storage. All other virtual machines are cloned from the base one by creating their own snapshots. Thus, all the clones may share the common blocks from the main storage image that remains unchanged. When booting up one virtual machine, shared blocks in the main image are cached via a page cache. As a result, physical disk accesses to the main image by other virtual machines can be greatly reduced.

We propose a novel method based on the snapshot method. Note that, when a virtual machine boots up the guest operation system, most disk blocks fetched to the memory will never be modified as long as the virtual machine is running. We can share such blocks each in a single physical memory page via the CoW (Copy on Write) mechanism. With the sharing, not only the disk accesses will be reduced, but also the total memory requirement is greatly reduced. Moreover, the CPU cache hit rates can be increased.

L. Boursas et al. (Eds.): SVM 2009, CCIS 71, pp. 67–74, 2010.

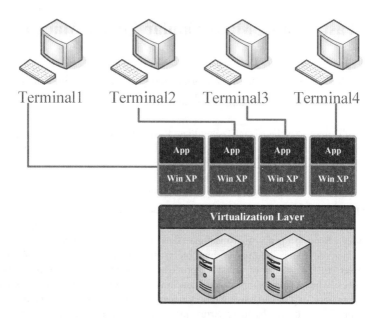

Fig. 1. Network classroom

We implement our method in KVM [4] with *Qcow* [5], a snapshot-enabled disk image type. In the rest of the paper, section 2 discusses the design issues; section 3 describes the implementation details, section 4 presents the experiment results, and finally, section 5 concludes with some discussions on our future work.

2   Design

When a series of similar virtual machines are booting up, a later one will read many identical disk blocks that the first virtual machine has already read into its memory. The goal of our method is to identify such disk reads and find out correspond memory pages in the first virtual machine, then map those pages to the later virtual machine and mark the page as CoW (Copy-on-Write) [6]. We call the process as *booting blocks sharing*. We use the *Qcow* format disk image to support this process. Figure 2 illustrates the two major modifications on KVM.

There are five steps generally to fulfill booting blocks sharing. The first step is to prepare a snapshot enabled virtual disk. We choose the Qcow image file as the virtual disk. The second step is to startup the source virtual machine. Disk blocks read by the source virtual machine can be shared through memory page mapping by those follow-ing virtual machines when they startup. The third step is to startup virtual machines that may share disk blocks. We intercept the disk I/O read operations and check whether to map a disk block already read as the response content and return. The fourth step is to process those share memory page so that all virtual machines may run properly. And the last step is to free those shared memory pages when all virtual ma-chines shutdown. We detail each step as following.

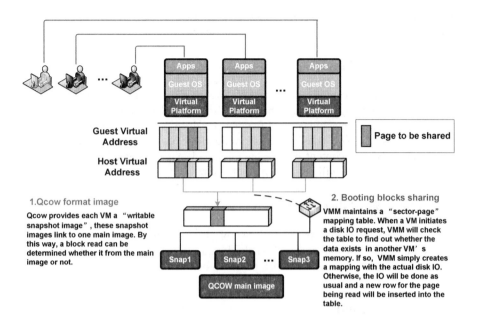

Fig. 2. Two modifications on KVM

2.1 Qcow Image File Type

Qcow is an image file type provided by QEMU. A snapshot Qcow image file reference a main Qcow image file while it itself only contains those changed data different from the main image file. A snapshot Qcow image file can be easily created from the main image. We duplicate a series of similar virtual machines by simply creating a group of snapshot Qcow image files from the main image. As a result, these virtual machines share many common data in the main image.

2.2 Starting Up the Source Virtual Machine

While booting a virtual machine, all blocks read from the main image are recorded to a sharable table. The sharable table works for holding the relationship between the sharable block and the memory page containing the block data. We can learn the relationship of block and block page right after the DMA operation complete, since if there is an enabled DMA, all disk reads are performed through it.

2.3 Starting Up Other Virtual Machines

While booting other similar virtual machines, sharable blocks that should be read from the main image might have been read into memory by previous booting up virtual machines. We could check whether there exists a sharable block page for the block through the sharable table before the block read request is sent to DMA. If the sharable block page exists, we can map the page for the virtual machine instead of sending the read request to DMA. Since disk read can be avoided by mapping sharable block page, booting process may be speed up correspondingly.

2.4 Sharing Block Pages

A sharable block page might be shared by two or more virtual machines. If one of them writes to the page, the page becomes dirty for all other virtual machines. To prevent other virtual machines from reading the dirty data, the sharable block page should be mark as CoW. Thus, once a sharable block page is updated, a new memory page is allocated, the content of the sharable block page is copied to the new page, and the write operation will be performed on the new page [7].

2.5 Freeing Shared Block Pages

When all virtual machines shutdown, sharable block pages should be free. A reference count can be maintained with each sharable block page. When the reference count drops to zero, the sharable block page can be freed.

3 Implementation

We implement our design in KVM-84. In KVM, a VM runs as a QEMU process in the host Linux. Most hardware devices are emulated in QEMU. We add a DRF (DMA Read Filter) module to the Qcow module in QEMU to monitor all disk reads, and add a SBM (Sharable Block Manager) module in the KVM module in order to help VMs share block pages.

3.1 DMA Read Filter

The DRF (DMA Read Filter) module is added to the Qcow module in QEMU to monitor all disk reads. When a VM initiates a disk read, a DMA read request will be sent to the Qcow module. The request contains the beginning sector number and the number of sectors to read, as well as the guest physical memory address where DMA will transfer disk block data to. DRF will filter such DMA read request before it reaches the Qcow module.

Most DMA reads are 8 sectors aligned, and only a few DMA reads request less than 8 sectors, so we group each aligned 8 sectors as a block. Since the content of a block will be filled in a whole memory page by DMA, we call the memory page as a block page after the DMA operation complete.

DRF will check all DMA read requests. If a block read by a VM targets the main image file, the block might be read again by another VM, thus, the block is a sharable block. DRF may check whether a sharable block is already read by another VM and the sharable block page is still available for mapping to the VM. If the sharable block page is available, DRF will not ask Qcow to read the block, instead, DRF will ask KVM to map sharable block pages directly to the VM. If the sharable block page is not available, DRF will let the request of the block pass through to Qcow. After Qcow completes the DMA read, the block data will be put in a memory page, and the memory page becomes a sharable block page. DRF will register the sharable block page to KVM for later querying and mapping.

If a requested block is read from the snapshot image file, then the block is not sharable. DRF left those block request pass thought to Qcow for further processing.

3.2 Sharable Block Manager

The SBM (Sharable Block Manager) module is added to the KVM module, which runs in host Linux kernel. SMB maintains a sharable table. The table records the relationships between sharable blocks and sharable block pages. If a sharable block page is shared by two VMs, the page will be marked as CoW. With CoW, once the page is modified by a write instruction, the content of the page will be copied to a new memory page, and the write will be executed on the new page.

Since QEMU runs as a user mode process, to enable the QEMU process to communicate with the KVM module, we create a special device in the KVM module. The QEMU process can open the device using a given name, and perform IOCTL operations on the device.

Two types of operations can be invoked though the device: *map_sharable_block_pages* and *register_sharable_block_pages*. When a VM send a disk read request to DMA, the request is filtered by DRF. DRF would identify all sharable blocks from the request, and call *map_sharable_block_pages* via IOCTL to KVM. Then in KVM, *map_sharable_block_pages* will check whether those sharable blocks are already registered in the sharable table, and, for the matched sharable block pages, mark these pages as CoW and map them to the request VM. Different from the memory mechanism of VMWare ESX server [8], if these memory region are changed by another I/O operation through QEMU, the CoW mechanism will take action.

DRF would send real DMA request to the lower level for those unmapped block. When all block data is available, DAI will register those sharable blocks read from the main image via *register_sharable_block_pages*. Then in KVM, *register_sharable_block_pages* will build up the relationship between the block and the block page, and record the relationship in the sharable table.

3.3 Monitoring Writes on Sharable Pages

Once the content of a sharable block page is modified, the page can no longer be a sharable block page, and should be removed from the sharable table.

In KVM, a VM accesses memory via a shadow page table, and the shadow page table is maintained by KVM. A shadow page entry is created until the VM read or write the memory page. The corresponding shadow page entry is cleared as soon as the page is marked as a sharable block page. Any write to the sharable block page will be captured by VMM, and then the page can be removed from the sharable table.

We implement the sharable table as a hash table. So that the average cost of looking up a block page is constant, and the size of the hash table is limited. For each record of a block page in the sharable table, there is an *is_alive* field, if the value of *is_alive* is *true*, the block page is sharable, if the value is set to *false*, then, the block is not sharable. So that, we don't have to really remove a modified block page from the sharable table, instead, simply mark the page as non-sharable.

4 Experiments

We design two experiments to verify our idea. In the first experiment, we boot up a group of similar virtual machines one by one; in the second experiment, those similar virtual machines are booted up all at once right after the first virtual machine boots up.

The experiment environment is described as follows. The computer is a personal computer with a 4-core Core 2 Q9550 CPU at 2.83GHz with a 12MB L2 cache, 8GB of main memory, and a 250GB 7200rpm SATA disk with a 2MB cache. The host Linux kernel version is 2.6.26.6. The KVM version is 84, and the Qcow image file type version is 1.

The guest OSes are Window XP SP2, and each virtual machine is assigned with 512MB memory and 10GB disk in the Qcow snapshot image file.

4.1 Boot Up One by One

In this experiment, we boot up similar virtual machines one by one and as many as possible. In order to guarantee that the next virtual machine starts to boot right after the previous one boots up, we add an auto run bat file in each virtual machine. The bat file would automatically start up the next virtual machine when the previous virtual machine boot up.

The experiment is repeated three times on the original KVM and on our modified KVM. We record the booting time (seconds) of each virtual machine in tables 1 and 2. In the original KVM, the first VM's booting time is not much difference from the second, third and fourth VM.

But in our modified KVM, the second, third and fourth VM's booting time is much less than the first VM's booting time. On the other hand, because we use CoW instead of disk I/O emulating, the machine memory saved could support more VMs running on the virtualization platform.

Booting time increases as the number of booted VMs grows, because free memory decreases in the same time. In the original KVM, when the 12th VM boot up, free memory left is not enough to allow any more VM to boot up. In our modified KVM, 2 more VMs can boot up than in the original KVM, since many memory pages are shared by VMs.

Table 1. Boot up one by one in the original KVM

Exp.No.	1st VM	2nd VM	3rd VM	4th VM	5th VM	6th VM	7th VM	8th VM	9th VM	10th VM	11th VM	12th VM
No.1	65s	61s	63s	68s	70s	71s	79s	83s	83s	87s	97s	102s
No.2	63s	66s	64s	69s	72s	75s	79s	86s	79s	93s	99s	96s
No.3	72s	69s	65s	72s	75s	72s	78s	83s	85s	89s	94s	104s
Avg	66.7s	65.3s	64s	69.7s	72.3s	73s	78.7s	84s	82.3s	89.7s	96.7s	100.7s
Role avg.	66.7s	79.7s										

Table 2. Boot up one by one in our modified KVM

Exp.No.	1st VM	2nd VM	3rd VM	4th VM	5th VM	6th VM	7th VM	8th VM	9th VM	10th VM	11th VM	12th VM	13th VM	14th VM
No.1	66s	31s	41s	47s	36s	34s	35s	39s	38s	40s	46s	49s	58s	61s
No.2	65s	37s	35s	33s	38s	37s	42s	39s	41s	45s	43s	49s	45s	59s
No.3	75s	33s	39s	40s	42s	36s	46s	42s	45s	42s	50s	51s	49s	62s
Avg	68.7s	34.7s	38.3s	40s	38s	35.7s	41s	40s	41.3s	42.3s	46.3s	49.7s	50.7s	60.7s
Role avg.	68.7s	42.7s												

The experiments show that, our method to reduce disk reads can speed up the booting process, and increase the number of VMs that can boot up.

4.2 Boot Up Simultaneously

In this experiment, the other VMs start to boot all together right after the first VM boot up. The experiment results are listed in tables 3 and 4.

In the original KVM, the following VMs spend much more time to boot up than the first VM, because these VMs interfere with each other when they access to the shared disk. In our modified KVM, the following VMs boot up much faster than the first VM.

Table 3. Boot up at once in the original KVM

Exp.No.	1st VM	2nd VM	3rd VM	4th VM	5th VM	6th VM	7th VM	8th VM	9th VM
No.1	71s	196s	185s	181s	227s	171s	204s	201s	223s
No.2	70s	187s	205s	169s	190s	212s	220s	218s	179s
No.3	66s	199s	182s	209s	231s	193s	188s	241s	185s
Avg	69s	194s	190.7s	186.3s	216s	192s	203s	220s	195.7s
Role avg.	69s	199.7s							

Table 4. Boot up at once in our modified KVM

Exp.No.	1st VM	2nd VM	3rd VM	4th VM	5th VM	6th VM	7th VM	8th VM	9th VM	10th VM	11th VM	12th VM
No.1	75s	69s	65s	110s	131s	119s	121s	139s	125s	97s	102s	117
No.2	62s	76s	98s	124s	106s	110s	127s	86s	133s	106s	99s	129
No.3	67s	120s	111s	135s	91s	94s	103s	107s	115s	122s	94s	104s
Avg	68s	88.3s	91.3s	123s	109.3s	107.7s	117s	110.7s	124.3s	108.3s	98.3s	116.7s
Role avg.	68s	108.6s										

In the original KVM, the maximum number of VMs that can boot up together after the first VM is 8. In our modified KVM, the maximum number of MVS is 12. Both numbers are less than in corresponding cases of booting up VMs one by one.

The experiments show that, our method does reduce many disk reads and speed up the booting process. But when disk block are not from the main image, the shared disk accessing is still the bottleneck of the booting process.

5 Conclusion

In many situations such as websites hosting and classroom teaching, when virtualization is applied, we need to boot up a series of similar virtual machines simultaneously.

Our idea of sharing common block data among virtual machines can remarkably speed up the booting process.

Our study is still preliminary. Our future work will investigate how to share the same content pages efficiently, how to monitor the shared page when apply EPT or NPT, and how to share block pages between the host and virtual machines, and so on.

Acknowledgement

This work is supported by the National Grand Fundamental Research 973 Program of China under Grant No.2007CB310900, National Science Foundation of China under Grant No.90718028 and No.60873052, National High Technology Research 863 Program of China under Grant No.2008AA01Z112, and MOE-Intel Information Technology Foundation under Grant No.MOE-INTEL-08-09. Zhenlin Wang is also supported by NSF Career CCF0643664. Corresponding author: Yingwei Luo, lyw@pku.edu.cn.

References

1. Seawright, L., MacKinnon, R.: VM/370, a study of multiplicity and usefulness. IBM Systems Journal 18, 4–17 (1979)
2. Barham, P., Dragovic, B., Fraser, K., Hand, S., Harris, T., Ho, A., Neugebauer, R., Pratt, I., Warfield, A.: Xen and the art of virtualization. In: Proceedings of the 19th ACM Symposium on Operating Systems Principles, pp. 164–177. ACM Press, New York (2003)
3. Rosenblum, M., Garfinkel, T.: Virtual Machine Monitors: Current Technology and Future Trends. IEEE Computer Magazine 38, 39–47 (2005)
4. KVM, http://www.linux-kvm.org/
5. Qcow format version 1, http://www.gnome.org/~markmc/qcow-image-format-version-1.html
6. Gorman, M.: Understanding the Linux Virtual Memory Manager. Prentice Hall PTR, Englewood Cliffs (2004)
7. Love, R.: Linux Kernel Development. Novell Press (2005)
8. Waldspurger, C.A.: Memory resource management in VMware ESX Server. In: Proceedings of the 5th Symposium on Operating Systems Design and Implementation, ACM SIGOPS Operating Systems Review, vol. 36, pp. 181–194. ACM Press, New York (2002)

On I/O Virtualization Management

Vitalian A. Danciu and Martin G. Metzker

Munich Network Management Team
Ludwig-Maximilians-Universität, Munich, Germany
{danciu,metzker}@mnm-team.org

Abstract. The quick adoption of virtualization technology in general and the advent of the Cloud business model entail new requirements on the structure and the configuration of back-end I/O systems. Several approaches to virtualization of I/O links are being introduced, which aim at implementing a more flexible I/O channel configuration without compromising performance. While previously the management of I/O devices could be limited to basic technical requirments (e.g. the establishment and termination of fixed-point links), the additional flexibility carries in its wake additional management requirements on the representation and control of I/O sub-systems.

This paper focuses on the modelling of dynamic and static aspects of the management of virtual I/O devices. Based on management scenarios and common operations on virtual machines we propose management function prototoypes and discuss the corresponding necessary information items.

1   Introduction

Consolidation of data centres and the introduction of massively virtualized system infrastructures have created new challenges to the construction and the management of I/O systems. The aggregation of data and thus I/O traffic and the need for flexible assignment of I/O capacity has given rise to the introduction of configurable I/O controllers and link schemes in order to replace the traditional, monolithic I/O setups. However, the flexibility introduced thereby necessarily introduces I/O facilities into the scope of IT management: while raw transmission capabilities were viable metrics before, management attention is shifting towards the configuration and setup issues arising from the need to apply the characteristics of these new devices to the emerging I/O usage scenarios.

Transition to virtualized sub-system elements. The I/O sub-system of computer systems relies on a fixed assignment of components, especially host bus adaptors (HBA), in order to exchange data with back-end remote systems, typically storage facilities. The I/O performance available to a computing resource (CR), which is either a physical or a virtual machine (VM), is therefore directly dependent on the capabilities of the hardware components of the I/O sub-system. In virtualized installations, multiple VMs share the same HBA; typically, I/O is being identified as a performance bottleneck in such installations.

L. Boursas et al. (Eds.): SVM 2009, CCIS 71, pp. 75–86, 2010.

To address these issues, hardware components have been developed to include multiple controller instances and to enable hardware accelerated I/O virtualization. Figure 1 shows the structural changes to the I/O sub-system in the transition from the non-virtualized to the virtualized I/O setup. Virtual HBAs (vHBA) are provided directly by the hardware, and the burden of assignment is placed on hypervisor functions.

Management problem. The introduction of these features entails novel management tasks: while before, the I/O sub-system could be viewed as a black box from an IT management standpoint, the newly won flexibility creates the need to extend management operations into the configuration of virtualization capable I/O devices. Even without taking into account changing user/customer requirements, the I/O capacity available to a VM is dependent on the number and the state of other VMs being supported on a given physical platform instance. While in a non-virtualized setup, I/O capacity planning for a machine was performed at the time of purchase (by selecting the machine hardware according to needs), system virtualization combined with I/O-virtualization allow—and mandate—the projection of management goals onto the I/O sub-system at run-time. The management operations necessary to realise that projection are important, as are the attributes required to represent the I/O sub-system's state. The formulation of such operations and information items must take into the account the fact that I/O virtualization is being introduced in several technically different manners and that the higher-level (i.e. application-driven) management goals to be achieved differ in the requirements they place on the management of the I/O sub-system.

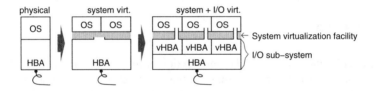

Fig. 1. Evolution from physical to virtual HBAs

Structure of this paper. In this paper, we derive management requirements regarding the configuration and operation of virtual I/O sub-system components from usage scenarios common in data centres. The requirements analysed in this paper and the therefrom derived model elements cover in principle both NICs and HBA. In the interest of clarity we will focus on HBAs.

We discuss management scenarios and analyse their requirements in Section 2 before reviewing different types of I/O virtualization and relevant standards in Section 3. According to these requirements we formulate management operations applicable to virtualizable I/O devices and identify the management information necessary in Section 4 to propose a sub-model aligned to the CIM. We conclude with a general discussion of this work in Section 5 and open questions in Section 6.

2   Management Scenario

A data centre operator rents out parts of his infrastructure to customers, thus providing quasi-isolated, virtual infrastructures. Simply speaking, the operator creates a number of VMs and assigns them to customers in accordance to provisioning contracts and service level agreements. Additionally, the operator offers storage resources that are made available to customers' VMs.

Management of these infrastructures aims to satisfy customer requirements while efficiently exploiting the operator's resources. Thus, higher-level management goals dictated by customer requirements lead to the execution of operations at the VM level and entail, as a direct consequence, requirements on the management of the I/O sub-systems.

Common operations on VMs (i.e. computing resources) include their instantiation/creation, the connection of data channels and, eventually, their disconnection as well as the decommisioning of the computing resource itself. When a multitude of similar VMs are required, VMs can be cloned from an existing blueprint instance. In addition, VMs can be migrated between physical machines, either while running or in a suspended state. Figure 2 shows an example sequence of such operations, that imply action items at the I/O sub-system level.

Computing units and storage space are connected by means of suitably dimensioned data channels in the operator's network (see Figure 3(a)). Thus, to provide service to a single group of computing resources, the provider must take into account the state of data channels (up, down, load etc), the endpoints of data channels and the service level constraints (gurantees regarding availability, thoughput, etc).

The provider reduces the number of running physical machines outside of peak usage periods in order to lower the energy expenditure for operation and cooling by consolidating VMs on fewer machines. However, the provider must ensure that their corresponding

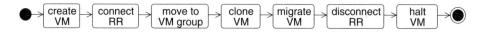

Fig. 2. Example life-cycle phases of VM

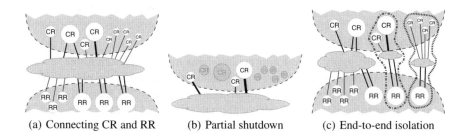

(a) Connecting CR and RR   (b) Partial shutdown   (c) End-to-end isolation

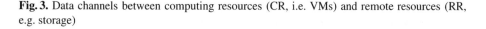

Fig. 3. Data channels between computing resources (CR, i.e. VMs) and remote resources (RR, e.g. storage)

data channels are reconfigured to operate to the same specifications as demanded by service level agreements (cp. Figure 3(b)).

The consolidation of multiple customers' VMs on the same machine pools implies potential security threats from the point of view of customers that perform computations on sensitive data. In the same manner, shared data channels to storage resources present (or may be seen to present, by co-hosted competitors in business) a similar risk. To guarantee isolation the provider must provide separate data channels between CR and RR (in addition to providing separate CR and RR) as depicted in Figure 3(c). The isolation of data links traversing the network is achieved by using separate virtual LANs (VLANs) for channels pertaining to one customer.

Management requirements. The provider faces several management challenges with respect to I/O management. It is notable that such requirements introduce the need to externalise part of the management functions to a manager component (or person).

placement and connection of CR and RR require management *information about the assignment* of VMs to I/O devices to be available, as well as *functions* to configure the I/O system.

group membership allow VMs and data channels to be included in unique logical groups, e.g. by customer, to enforce isolation requirements;

isolation requires that the assignment operations must take into account the *mapping of VM groups* to different customers, the *criticality and sensitivity* stated in customers' contracts in addition to quality of service requirements.

temporary re-location in order to lower the physical infrastructure's energy footprint requires functions for the *re-configuration* of CR–to–RR connections.

transit constraints forbid data (or VM migration) transit through a given network (e.g. over the internet); or mandate transit over a specific network;

capacity guarantees state a capacity (e.g. transmission rate) guaranteed to customer (while this requirement may be fulfilled automatically in a static environment, its fulfilment needs to be revised in the context of changes to VM deployment such as migration, cloning, re-configuration of channels etc);

redundancy guarantees state a measure of redundancy guaranteed to be provided, e.g. a customer may require double the number of effectively needed communication channels to allow for failover. Again, this last requirement breaks the encapsulation provided by I/O virtualization: if redundancy is to protect against faults in hardware, there is little point in providing two different virtual entities that are dependent on the same physical entity; a direct view into the mappings of virtual devices to physical ones is necessary to fulfil such a requirement by assigning redundant *physical* channels.

These requirements imply several information items that are relevant to the scenarios discussed, but not in the scope of the model elements describing the management of I/O devices: they are instead a source of constraints and goals (e.g. constraints/policies derived from customers' requirements, or formulated in SLAs/SLOs) with respect to that management. Methods for the detailed, formal description of the constraints themselves constitute interesting research items but fall outside the scope of this paper. We will refer to a set of constraints available to the provider, and we take them into account as a whole when treating functions and information items.

3   Background

The virtualization of the I/O sub-system borders, as a topic, on several different areas including data-centre-grade interconnects, the means of virtualization employed, and the resulting virtual structures in terms of networks, links and endpoints.

I/O virtualization techniques. I/O virtualization is being realised either in the hardware platform (i.e. as CPU functions), in the system bus, within the HBA or as a specialised I/O Server, as sketched in Figure 4. An example for platform-based implementation is Intel's VT-d [2] which creates an abstraction from concrete data channels by allowing a re-mapping of DMA (direct memory access) transfers and of the interrupts generated by the I/O device. In contrast, an example for HBA-based I/O virtualization is found in the SR-IOV (Single-Root I/O Virtualisation) [9] extension of the PCI-Express [8] system bus.

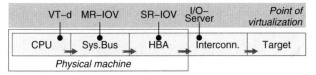

Fig. 4. Different points of virtualization on transmission path

An SR-IOV-capable HBA provides "virtual functions" that mimic multiple devices on the PCI bus that can be separately assigned to computing resources. MR-IOV (Multi-Root IOV) [10] virtualizes switch-based PCI Express topologies with multiple root entities, as found in blade installations. I/O servers externalise I/O devices into an entity outside the host machine and offer virtual HBA instances as a service. It is obvious that, while the goal of I/O virtualization remains the same, the means of realisation are quite different.

Management of I/O virtualization. By using specialized components, virtualization can be implemented more efficiently. On the other hand it requires the orchestration of multiple functions of different entities to supply a (virtual) machine with an HBA, making it harder to describe a (virtual) machine's setup. Similar problems arise when creating virtual networks across large infrastructures, as described in [5], that describes a method for instantiating and deploying security and isolation mechanisms in virtualized environments. Rooney et al. describe a method for automatic VLAN creation, based on on-line measurement [11], while [3] describes a resource provisioning scheme regarding resource availability. These technologies can simplify network management when combined to automatically instantiate and control data channels in a virtualized environment.

Operations on VMs must also respect a number of management policies and constraints, including the available system resources at specific locations in the infrastructure, the adherence to isolation of customers' VMs etc. These items constitute management challenges in their own right, but they are outside the scope of this paper; an overview may be found in [6].

4   Modelling Management Aspects

The scenarios' use-cases and the general management requirements discussion above incorporate a number of distinct physical and logical entities (see Figure 5 and Table 1) which are the target of management operations; where available we have leveraged existing CIM classes to represent these entities.

We extend the CIM PortController class by deriving a new class, VirtualPortController, to integrate a virtual I/O device into a virtual machine's model without having to modify other aspects of its model. The accompanying classes PortControllerFactory and VirtualizationFacility are used to model virtualization capabilities. VirtualizationFacility represents the device that provides virtual instances, while PortControllerFactory is the managing class which controls and monitors such instances.

4.1   I/O Sub-system Management Functions

Figure 6 shows the sequence of basic functions for the management of virtual I/O channels as needed in the use-cases in Section 2: the creation of a VM, the initialization of

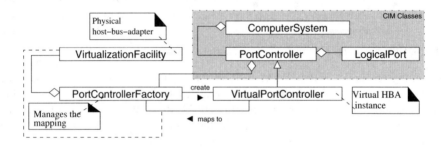

Fig. 5. Model view of the basic virtulization function

Table 1. Entity classes

Class	Description
PortController	respresents a *physical HBA* with the ability to create a comm. end-point
VirtualPortController	represents a *virtual HBA*; its exposed functions correspond to, and are mapped to, those of a physical HBA
PortControllerFactory	is an entity that instatiates *VirtualPortController* instances on a *PortController* with the aid of a *VirtualizationFacility*. This entity encapsulates the basic management functions for creation of virtual I/O devices (vHBAs, virtual NICs etc). Its functions may be provided by hypervisor software.
VirtualizationFacility	represents the (physical) device that provides the virtualization function, i.e. one of the devices realising the virtualization points shown in Figure 4
Manager	an entity that enforces management policy by executing actions on the I/O devices (cp. Figure 6)
Data channel	a link between two communication end-points, managed by two (virtual) Port-Controllers, e.g. a VLAN
ConstraintSet	contains the conditions that I/O channel operations must satisfy (in this paper, we use group membership as an example constraint)

a connection to a RR, as well as the subsequent disconnection of the resource and the decommissioning of the VM.

The task of creating a VM can be decomposed into single interactions. Note that a dominating aspect is the propagation of constraints. Distributing constraints top-down indicates that all key information lies with the Infrastructure-Manager, making this a very important (and busy) role throughout the VM's life-cycle. This is emphasised by the many tasks performed by the Infrastructure-Manager when connecting to a RR. The main objective in this phase is the mapping to a virtual network.

We have summarised the necessary operations in Table 2 together with descriptions of their effect. The operation signatures are grouped by the entities they pertain to, i.e. the classes that implement the operations.

Application to the examplary life-cycle phases. We compose the operations on VMs (e.g. those shown in the exemplary life-cycle in Figure 2) based on the primitive function blocks from the sequence diagram in Figure 6; note that some of the life-cycle phases can be mapped directly.

create VM. corresponds to the sequence shown in Figure 6.
connect RR. corresponds to the sequence shown in Figure 6
move to VM group. Assigning a VM to a group implies the specification of the policy of that group to be valid to the VM. The management actions required depend on

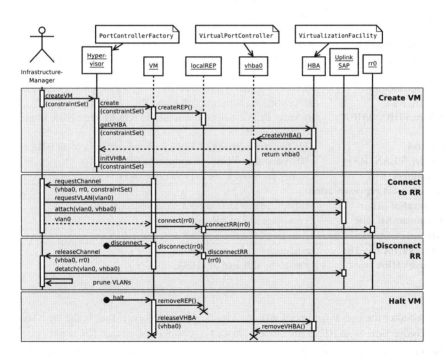

Fig. 6. Operations sequence during a VM's life-cycle

Table 2. Management operations, arranged by entity

Infrastructure Manager	
createVM (constraintSet)	Called by the manager to create a new virtual machine. The supplied constraintSet contains information controlling the I/O channels the VM will use.
requestVLAN (VLAN)	Used by the manager to configure the infrastructure.
attach (VLAN, vHBA)	Allows vHBA to access VLAN.
detach (VLAN,vHBA)	Reconfigures the infrastructure to deny vHBA access to VLAN.
pruneVLANs (void)	Cleanup function to remove unused VLANs from the infrastructure.
Hypervisor	
create (constraintSet)	This is the internal function used by the hypervisor to instantiate a new virtual machine.
getVHBA (constraintSet)	A call to this function makes the VirtualizationFacility create a new vHBA which will be used to access the network and configures the associated physical HBA. The supplied constraintSet influences the decision which physical HBA is mapped to.
initVHBA (constraintSet)	Binds a virtual HBA to a virtual machine and initiates the vHBA's identifying properties.
Virtual Machine	
createREP (void)	Creates the virtual machine's local representation of an HBA. The resulting object is used to interface the virtual hardware, supplied by the hypervisor.
removeREP (void)	Disconnects the local HBA representation from the associated vHBA and removes the representation.
requestChannel (vHBA, RR, constraintSet)	Prompts the manager for the VLAN which will be used by the supplied vHBA instance to access the supplied RR, taking into account constraintSet.
releaseChannel (vHBA, RR)	Prompts the manager to undo all configuration changes related to the connection between vHBA and RR.
releaseVHBA (vHBA)	Instructs the VirtualizationFacility to remove the vHBA when it is no longer used.
connect (vHBA, VLAN, RR)	This function binds the VM's local representation of an HBA to vHBA and uses VLAN to connect to RR.
disconnect (RR)	Locally unmount from RR and disconnect.
OS-side port representation	
connectRR (RR)	Initiates the connection between a VM and a RR.
disconnectRR (RR)	Terminates link to RR.
HBA	
createVHBA (void)	Instantiates a new virtual HBA.
removeVHBA (void)	Delete's an instance of vHBA.

whether the pre-assignment settings violate group policy. If that is the case for any connection to an RR, a disconnection and re-connection to that RR is necessary.

clone. Cloning a VM implies creating an additional instance with a disjunct identity but with the same configuration settings. In our context, this means that the new clone must hold equal connections to the I/O sub-system and respect the same constraints, but that these connections may have to be duplicated. Thus, the clone phase implies a disconnection of the resources bound to the clone blueprint and a re-connection performed by the new clone, i.e. instantiating a VirtualPortController and requesting it be placed into the same interconnect group as its sibling.

migrate. Migration implies that a VM is moved to another physical machine. There, it may or may not be offered the same I/O sub-system type and capabilities. To ensure the conservation of the CR–RR connection's parameters, bindings should be released before migration (i.e. disconnection sequences for all RRs) and re-constituted (connect sequences for all RRs) after migration is complete.

disconnect RR is shown in Figure 6

halt VM. Destruction/deletion of a VM corresponds to decommisioning according to Figure 6, followed by the release of other resources than those of the I/O sub-system and, finally, halting and deleting the VM.

4.2 Attributes

Taking into account the different alternatives for virtualizing I/O adaptors in a generic model representation has required the introduction of new entities for which we propose partial models in the following and consider the management elements external to the virtualization function, e.g. management goals to be attained by means of I/O virtualization control and the manager actor (the latter is detailed in Section 5).

Typically, the VirtualizationFacility is a hardware-based device that allows the projection of multiple logical derived devices. To administrate these derived (i.e. virtual devices), it is important to provide a counter of instantiated devices as well as information regarding the virtualization method used and the maximum number of virtual devices supported by the VirtualizationFacility (Figure 7(a)).

The PortControllerFactory (PCF) is responsible for creating virtual PortController instances based on the abilities of the VirtualizationFacility. In simple cases, the PCF may be a part of the hypervisor code; in other cases it may be a management function of a product supporting I/O virtualization (e.g. a physical HBA). Its primary task is to create and administrate VirtualPortController instances and to bind them to Logical-Port instances. There are conceivable environments in which machines equipped with virtualization-capable I/O devices and machines without those capabilities are mixed. Thus, to provide a robust representation of the PCF, it must be assigned at least one Port-Controller, whether it be a physical or a virtual instance. In case of a virtual instance,

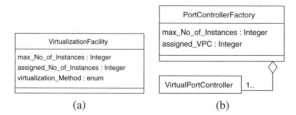

(a)   (b)

Fig. 7. Class attributes

that first PortController will simply serve as the first (perhaps of many) instances created; in case of a physical instance, it will ensure an appropriate interface to (an equally physical) LogicalPort. In the more interesting case, i.e. when I/O virtualization capabilities are present, the PCF must keep a list of managed VirtualPortControllers as well as suitable counter variables (Figure 7(b)).

5 Discussion

Substantial challenges to the management of the I/O sub-system originate in the variety of the infrastructure partitions, the differences in their use, the variance of usage over time ("burstiness") and, finally, the service levels assured to the customers. These are understood challenges in network management. Several common-sense principles may be employed to simplify infrastructure design and management [4]. *Uniformity* regarding the view on devices and configurations requires the bridging of heterogenity. The introduction of *roles* helps ease the configuration of components by splitting configurations into small units that can be reused on multiple components, thus reducing the number of special cases. Our approach attempts to serve these two principles by mapping the operations on VMs onto operations on the I/O sub-system in a generic manner, agnostic of the concrete I/O virtualization technology and of the point of its introduction on the data tranfer path.

Another important principle is the organisation of components into a *tiered structure* (instead of in a flat one) to enable operators to assign tasks to groups of elements, thus reducing the number of tasks per elements. The organisation of VMs (and VM groups) and virtual and physical I/O devices lends itself to such organisation inherently. A principle more difficult to preserve is that of keeping *short dependency chains* to allow a reduction of the side effect of management operations. This is due to the conditions imposed on the management of virtual I/O devices by external entities (provider's policy, customers' requirements etc). We have localised the responsibility for creating the link between internal and external aspects in the Infrastructure-Manager role.

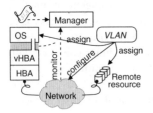

Fig. 8. Projecting management goals

The Infrastructure-Manager coordinates the steps when managing virtual infrastructures. While the effective configuration and orchestration can be automated, the Infrastructure-Manager has to supply the components with data on which resources to allocate and use. Often a human role is involved when grouping virtual machines and assigning resources. In particular, the Infrastructure-Manager role must have access to the policy set applicable to an infrastructure partition, for example a VM group, associated back-end storage, and the entities creating the data channel between the two. Thus, the manager's characteristic task in the context of virtualized I/O devices is to provide information *external* to that context. The application of that information is enacted by the *choice* of operations and attributes, instead of by relaying selected information to the acting entities (VirtualizationFacility, PortControllerFactory etc). Figure 8 shows the data flow to and from the manager entity and reflects the projection of (formalised) management goals on the execution of operations, by means of the example of VLAN assignment (from Figure 6).

Automation of the Infrastructure-Manager's tasks would imply their execution under a chosen control paradigm. Several approaches lend themselves to this task, among them policy-based and constraint based management. The formulation of rules with respect to I/O sub-system configuration appears to be a powerful means to manage data channels; however, the well-known issues of rule refinement and conflict handling must be considered.

6 Conclusion

The virtualization of I/O devices is a viable technology candidate to solve the I/O performance issues encountered in the heavily virtualized computing environments. We have analysed the management challenges posed by HBA virtualization scenarios and addressed the resulting requirements by identifying the management information necessary to perform the operations needed in the scenarios. We have covered a number of characteristic use-cases of HBA virtualization to identify the management functions and information items necessary at different points in the infrastructure.

This work ist but a step on the way towards consistent management of virtualized I/O devices: hardware products are still in development, and it remains to see which approach(es), as described in Section 3, will become dominant in the market. The multiple possible combinations of network protocols allow (virtual) I/O sub-systems different capabilities which in turn reflect on the management operations; an obvious example is the use of protocol stacks with QoS capabilities that allow effective management of data channel characteristics with respect to data rates, throughput and so on.

Acknowledgment

The authors wish to thank the members of the Munich Network Management Team (MNM Team) for helpful discussions and valuable comments on previous versions of this paper. The MNM Team directed by Prof. Dr. Dieter Kranzlmüller and Prof. Dr. Heinz-Gerd Hegering is a group of researchers at Ludwig-Maximilians-Universität München, Technische Universität München, the University of the Federal Armed Forces and the Leibniz Supercomputing Centre of the Bavarian Academy of Science. http://www.mnm-team.org.

References

1. Host LAN network port profile. Specification DSP1035, DMTF (April 2006)
2. Intel Virtualization Technology for Directed I/O (VT-d): Enhancing Intel platforms for efficient virtualization of I/O devices (August 2008),
   http://software.intel.com/en-us/articles/intel-
   virtualization-technology-for-directed-io-vt-d-enhancing-
   intel-platforms-for-efficient-virtualization-of-io-devices/
3. Ahmad, S.Z., Qadir, M.A., Akbar, M.S.: A distributed resource management scheme for load-balanced QoS provisioning in heterogeneous mobile wireless networks. In: Q2SWinet 2008: Proceedings of the 4th ACM symposium on QoS and security for wireless and mobile networks, pp. 63–70. ACM, New York (2008)

4. Benson, T., Akella, A., Maltz, D.: A case for complexity models in network design and management. Technical Report 1643, University of Wisconsin (August 2008)
5. Cabuk, S., Dalton, C.I., Ramasamy, H.G., Schunter, M.: Towards automated provisioning of secure virtualized networks. In: CCS 2007: Proceedings of the 14th ACM conference on Computer and communications security, pp. 235–245. ACM, New York (2007)
6. Danciu, V.A.: Host virtualization: a taxonomy of management challenges. In: SPIRIT 2009, Proceedings of the 2nd Workshop on Services, Platforms, Innovations and Research for new Infrastructures in Telecommunications, September 2009, Gesellschaft für Informatik (2009)
7. Metzker, M.: Design and analysis of techniques for virtualizing I/O-channels (in german). Master's thesis, Technical University Munich (April 2009)
8. PCI-SIG. PCI Express Base Specification Revision 2.0(December 2006)
9. PCI-SIG. Single Root I/O Virtualization and Sharing Specification Revision 1.0 (September 2007)
10. PCI-SIG. Multi-Root I/O Virtualization and Sharing Specification Revision 1.0 (May 2008)
11. Rooney, S., Hörtnagl, C., Krause, J.: Automatic VLAN creation based on on-line measurement. SIGCOMM Comput. Commun. Rev. 29(3), 50–57 (1999)
12. Storage Network Industry Association. Storage Management Initiative Specification (SMI-S), Version 1.4.0, Revision 4 (April 2009)

Availability Management in a Virtualized World

Chun-Shi Chang, Dave V. Bostjancic, and Michael D. Williams

IBM, 2455 South Rd, Poughkeepsie, NY 12601, USA
{chunshi,dbostjan,mdw}@us.ibm.com

Abstract. Virtualization technology is offering new and unique ways to better manage systems and the application workloads they support. In fact, virtualization is moving beyond single systems to pools of systems that can be logically managed as a single system in the data center. Virtualization also introduces a paradigm shift in availability management which significantly simplifies the complexity involved in achieving resiliency. The focus of this paper is to describe an availability management architecture, and discuss capabilities that can be used to provide virtual machine resiliency in today's virtualized data center. This paper addresses the detection and recovery of unplanned downtime resulting from system failures. In addition, we show that improved resiliency can be provided to virtual machines to minimize what has been traditional considered planned downtime.

Keywords: Availability, Virtualization.

1 Introduction

As virtualization technology gains in popularity, it has introduced a paradigm shift in availability management. Traditionally, high availability (HA) solutions require complex configurations performed by skilled specialists who have in depth knowledge of applications. A lengthy test period is typically required to validate a solution. The complexity and cost involved have become prohibiting factors in the adoption of HA solutions. However, with virtualization, the tasks required to achieve HA is significantly simplified. There is typically only one application which needs to be made highly available – the virtual machine. All I/O operations by applications running inside a virtual machine are monitored and recorded by a single entity, the virtual machine monitor. Any journal data needed for recovery actions can be retrieved from one place. In addition, there is no need of special HA configuration as a guest OS will handle all dependencies and bring up applications normally after virtual machine restarted.

In this paper, we present an availability management (AM) design that takes advantage of the paradigm shift. Such an AM system is essential to any next generation virtualization management discipline. With the new virtualization management technologies that are emerging, physical systems could be pooled together and managed as a single entity. A system pool represents a new type of system where a collection of virtual machines can be deployed to run user applications. This single entity view provides a level of simplification and optimization that cannot be achieved if systems

L. Boursas et al. (Eds.): SVM 2009, CCIS 71, pp. 87–93, 2010.
© Springer-Verlag Berlin Heidelberg 2010

are managed individually. The proposed AM design offers policy-base availability management capabilities. It is loosely based on the virtual availability manager (VAM) in IBM Systems Director Virtualization Manager 2.1 [1], but otherwise the design is completely new to align it with the new paradigm and the emerging virtualization management technologies.

The rest of this paper is organized as follows: The architecture of the proposed availability management design is described in section 2. AM is composed of three integral parts: availability configuration, monitoring technologies, and recovery capabilities, which are discussed in sections 3, 4, and 5, respectively. Conclusions are presented in section 6.

2   Availability Management Architecture

A virtualization management disciple D can be described as a 4-tuple

$D = \{M, P, V, I\}$

where

- P is set of zero or more physical systems,
- V denotes a set of zero or more virtual machines. Virtual machines have no fixed affinity with physical systems. In fact, virtual machines do not necessarily know nor care which physical machine they are running on.
- M represents the management entity to oversee P and V.
- I denotes interconnect, networks, shared storage devices, etc., between M, P, and V.

Availability management (AM) component is part of M, which runs on a set of machines that do not belong to P. The primary reason for M to run on more than one machines is to ensure HA of M. M provides a GUI for users to enter administrative requests, and for displaying status as well as topology of P and V. Among other functions, M also decides placement of virtual machines, and coordinate the movement of virtual machines from one physical system to another.

Figure 1 illustrates the components of the proposed virtualization management offering, with emphasis on availability related sub-systems. From a management console GUI, user can specify availability policy for a collection of virtual machines in a system pool. Based on the policy, AM monitors the health of systems, both physical and virtual, using a set of monitoring technologies. When events indicate systems are about to fail or have failed, AM invokes placement service [2] to formulate and execute recovery plans according to availability policy. A recovery plan is carried out through a series of calls to platform-agnostic service interfaces to place virtual machines within system pool. Platform-specific implementations of the service interfaces then drive the actions down to the end systems. This architecture allows the flexibility of adding additional platform supports as plugins.

While system faults put a system pool in a constrained state, and service interruption is inevitable; the recovery plan execution could remove the constraints and restore system pool back to equilibrium. The availability configuration, monitoring

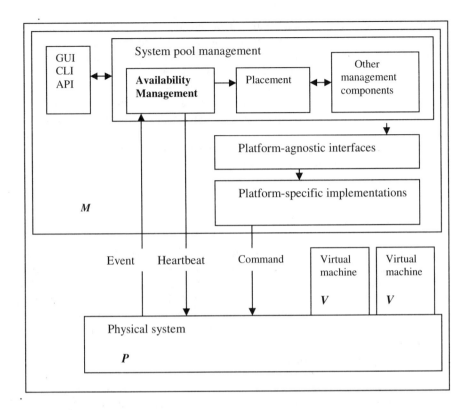

Fig. 1. Components in a proposed virtualization management discipline

technologies, and recovery capabilities form the three pillars of the proposed availability management system. We discuss the three pillars in the next three sections.

3 Availability Configuration

In the proposed AM system, availability configuration allows users to specify, at very high level, the course of actions AM should take to mitigate system failures. In current design, configuration is simplified so that it only requires the setting of a few control parameters. This should significantly reduce availability management complexity.

Table 1. Availability policy

Control parameters	Possible values		
Availability functionality	Off	On	
Additional availability function	-	Off	On
User confirmation	Off	On	

Table 1 shows the proposed control parameters and their possible values. The scope of the parameters should be a collection of virtual machines specified by user. When "Availability functionality" is set of "Off", AM will not take any recovery actions. However, when it is set to "On", AM will monitor physical system operating status, and attempt to recover from any physical system failure. Also, for each "Additional availability function", such as virtual machines failure recovery, there will be one control parameter which can be turned on individually. Separately, if "User confirmation" is set to "On", user's approval is required before any actions can be taken. An "Off" setting indicates actions can be taken automatically by AM. This user confirmation feature is provided so that user will have opportunities to validate actions proposed by AM before proceeding.

4   Monitoring Technologies

The capability of an HA system is ultimately limited by its abilities to detect system failures. The difficulty lies in the fact that it has to be done without missing a system failure, and without falsely reporting a system as failed while the system is healthy. As mentioned before, one of the primary goals of AM is to ensure virtual machines are continuously available. To accomplish the goal, the proposed AM system employs two levels of monitoring, physical system monitoring and virtual machine monitoring.

4.1   Physical System Monitoring

Physical system monitoring is essential for availability support in virtualized environments because of one important reason: Each physical system is a single point of failure for all virtual machines running on it. In this section, we propose three physical system monitoring mechanisms for AM: predictive failure analysis, heartbeat, and watchdog timer.

Predictive failure analysis. Predictive Failure Analysis (PFA) represents the ability given to key components in IBM servers to monitor their own health and generate an alert before failure actually occurs [3]. The PFA code monitors subsystems within a key component. If observed operation parameters exceed a pre-determined range, then an alert is generated. Such alerts typically will be converted to CIM indications, which can then be delivered to any interested parties.

Heartbeat. With the heartbeat approach, simple ICMP "echo request" packet (ping) will be sent to each physical system periodically. If a number of consecutive 'echo response' are missing from a system, the system is considered as unreachable. Since ping is a lightweight protocol, this approach is potentially scalable. However, if there is only one network connection from AM to a physical system, this approach has a drawback of not able to distinguish network failure from system failure. For this reason, this approach should be used only in the environment where multiple network connections exist to each system.

Watchdog timer. Watchdog timer is a common feature in enterprise-class servers [4]. A watchdog timer running on system service processor needs to be reloaded at fixed interval to prevent it from expiring. The reloading is typically done by a user space long running process. If a physical system is experiencing problems, which prevents the process from reloading watchdog timer, a timer will expire and automatically generate a previously configured action. Such an action could be to reboot the system, and it produces a clear indication that a physical system has gone down and lost all virtual machines running on it.

4.2 Virtual Machines Monitoring

One principle we adopted in AM design is to avoid the installation of 'agent' into virtual machine guest OS. This approach simplifies the administrative tasks needed for AM configuration, but it also implies to monitor the states of virtual machines, an outside agent using indirect data is required. We briefly discuss one such approach - machine learning – in this subsection.

Machine learning technology. Machine learning collects standard virtual machine operational metrics from hypervisor, and processes the data using statistical methods to produce classifiers [5]. A classifier is a piece of software that can be used to identify if a virtual machine is in normal or faulty state. In practice, classifiers are given real time data from live virtual machines and it uses the data to determine the current states of those virtual machines. This technology has demonstrated high classification accuracy over a diverse set of test data.

5 Recovery Capabilities

The primary goal of AM recovery capabilities is to reduce system downtime. System could become unavailable because of normal planned operations such as software update. Unplanned events such as hardware failure would also cause system outage. This section discusses the recovery capabilities offered by AM to handle both situations.

5.1 Planned System Outage

There are situations when a physical system needs to be made unavailable for normal operations. In this case, live migration of virtual machines will be invoked to minimize interruption in workload. The system will be placed in "Maintenance" mode, so no additional virtual machine will be deployed to it, and user will have opportunity to service the system. After service, the system should be put back to operating state, and ready for deployment of workload.

5.2 Unplanned System Outage

Depending on the failure indications from different monitoring technologies (see section 4), AM would employ different recovery methods.

Live migration of virtual machines. This mode of recovery is possible only for predictive failure analysis events. When PFA event occurs, system could stay up for a period of time before failure actually happens, hence live migration of virtual machines can be triggered to move them to back up systems. The failing system will be placed in "Maintenance" mode, so no virtual machine will be deployed to it, and user will have opportunity to service the faulty system. After service, the system should be put back to operating state, and ready for deployment of workload.

Remote restart of virtual machines. This recovery capability will be invoked when heartbeat or watchdog timer reports hard system failure. Since the original system is down, the virtual machines that used to be running there need to be restarted somewhere else. Essentially, the following steps need to be taken:

1. Retrieve profile of a virtual machine from persistent database.
2. Create a virtual machine on backup system using the retrieved profile. It is critical that the virtual machine image be reside on a shared storage device accessible by the original and backup systems.
3. Start the created virtual machine from a consistent state off the virtual machine image.

Local restart of virtual machines. When machine learning reports a virtual machine failure, AM will restart the virtual machine locally on the same system. In current proposal, the recovery mechanisms are reboot and re-initialization of the virtual system.

6 Conclusion

The system pool concept represents a natural next step in the evolution of virtualization management. A system pool with continuous availability support provides a robust infrastructure on which data center can be built and compute cloud can be deployed. This paper presents an availability management system that provides continuous availability support for virtual machines in system pool environment [6]. It is based on proven, leading-edge technologies, and it embraces the availability-via-virtualization paradigm. We believe the resulting product when delivered will bring new levels of simplicity and affordability to availability management.

In the future, we plan to extend our AM system to support disaster recovery where system pools at geographically dispersed locations can back up each other. We also plan to introduce memory and data checkpoint capabilities into the system, so in case of failure, virtual machine could restart from checkpoint.

References

1. International Business Machines Corporation. IBM Systems Director Virtualization Manager Version 1 Release 2 (2007),
   http://publib.boulder.ibm.com/infocenter/eserver/v1r2/topic/eica7/eica7.pdf
2. Tang, C., Steinder, M., Spreitzer, M., Pacifici, G.: A Scalable Application Placement Controller for Enterprise Data Centers. In: WWW 2007 (2007)

3. International Business Machines Corporation, Predictive Failure Analysis,
   `http://www-05.ibm.com/hu/termekismertetok/xseries/dn/pfa.pdf`
4. Intel Corporation, Hewlett-Packard Company, NEC Corporation, Dell Inc.: Intelligent
   Platform Management Interface Specification, Second Generation V2.0, Document revision
   1.0 (2006)
5. Pelleg, D., Ben-Yehuda, M., Harper, R.E., Spainhower, L., Adeshiyan, T.O.S.: Vigilant:
   Out-of-Band Detection of Failures in Virtual Machines. ACM SIGOPS Operating Systems
   Review 42(1), 26–31 (2008)
6. Farr, E.M., Harper, R.E., Spainhower, L.F., Xenidis, J.: A Case for High Availability in a
   Virtualized Environment (HAVEN). In: Proceedings of the Third International Conference
   on Availability, Reliability and Security, ARES 2008, pp. 675–682. IEEE, New York (2008)

Enhancing Trust in SOA Based Collaborative Environments

Latifa Boursas[1], Mohamed Bourimi[2],
Wolfgang Hommel[3], and Dogan Kesdogan[4]

[1] Munich University of Technology, Germany
Munich Network Management Team
boursas@tum.de
[2] FernUniversitt in Hagen, Germany
mohamed.bourimi@fernuni-hagen.de
[3] Leibniz Supercomputing Centre, Germany
Munich Network Management Team
hommel@lrz.de
[4] University of Siegen, Germany
kesdogan@fb5.uni-siegen.de

Abstract. Considering trust and privacy requirements for online and collaborative distance learning environments, this paper discusses potential extensions of SOA based applications to simultaneously support authentication and authorization services, and offering mutual trust to both learners and service providers. This study shows that the security mechanisms integrated in the SOA platform can be effectively extended and correlated with a trust model.

1 Introduction

The recent massive growth of the web-based businesses gains strength from leveraging efficient communication patterns and tight seamlessly IT-supported collaboration between organizations as well as communities. It is part of a major effort to improve the IT's alignment with the business processes and to remain competitive on the market. As a result, supporting business processes with information technology among several organizations is now – from a technical perspective – on the edge of enabling us to successfully be able to treat inter-organizational scenarios just like one large integrated enterprise.

Interorganizational scenarios can – in a simplified manner – be defined as a collection of services from providers that are situated in different management domains and exchange messages with each other to achieve a common task in an orchestrated manner. The communication in this regard can involve either simple payload data passing, or it involves two or more services coordinating some activity, i.e. the exchange of meta-data, e.g. as a part of negotiation protocol phases. Service-Oriented Architectures (SOA) and Web-Oriented Architectures (WOA) are employed for these coordination tasks and aim for a wide range of web-based and web-services-based applications.

L. Boursas et al. (Eds.): SVM 2009, CCIS 71, pp. 94–102, 2010.

However, as information can be transmitted between the involved parties through the coupled services, enhancing *trust* among the collaborative partners as well as respecting the privacy constraints when exchanging customers' sensitive data need to be handled with special care. Service Level Agreements (SLAs) are employed in inter-organizational scenarios to guarantee service provision and resource sharing while protecting those same resources from unauthorized access, but they are paperware documents and thus very static. As a fatal consequence, the purely SLA-based approach fails to fulfill various important requirements that dominate highly dynamic real-world scenarios.

The goal of establishing trust efficiently in dynamic environments requires adaptations and extensions of the overall Service Level Management (SLM) process. For example, new measures for keeping track of participants' behavior, and assessing their trustworthiness in accordance with the underlying business and collaboration agreements are required. To investigate how SOA applications can be extended with a trust management (TM) process, in Section 2 this paper sheds some light on a real-world scenario to outline some TM problems that interorganisational scenarios are faced with. An overview on related work is given in Section 3. Next, Section 4 presents our solution for integrating the trust model in SOA applications. Finally, we conclude with an overview on possible extensions and future work in Section 5.

2   Scenario

In this section, we present a simplified interorganizational distance learning scenario that highlights some of the key requirements for a TM process. The objective therein is to provide the students with shared workspaces in the effort of reducing classroom and building requirements, as well as reducing inventories of books and libraries.

In our scenario, such a workspace, based on the learning material provided by different eLearning service providers, is represented in the CURE system [7] that supports an innovative didactic approach called self-organized learning. One of the major features of this system is the personalization of learning paths, so that a central authority manages the learning material, because the CURE systems is based on a star topology where the main collaborative platform represents the central node and the end-users' host using web browser represent the surrounding nodes.

As illustrated in Figure 1, for example, the students seeking to acquire some learning material for a given demonstration course have the possibility to select the appropriate service providers according to the information available on their web sites on the client side, and subsequently by using the search and comparison reports of the CURE system based on the SOA platform. The result of the search from the CURE Web Server obviously may involve several service providers in order to elect the desired learning material, building thus a learning path among the involved providers. Such a learning path may include, for example, a content provider as well as a publishing provider that publishes the learning course stored in the content provider and that provides remote access to it.

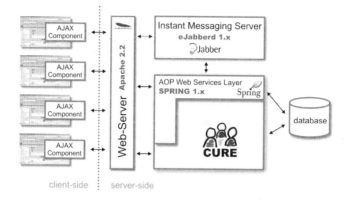

Fig. 1. System architecture of the retrofitted CURE system and its ubiquitous components

However, the choice of most suitable learning material becomes a controversial question due to the differences between the service providers that participate in the learning workspace. That is because, there is no mechanism that could report on which service provider is more reliable, for example in answering a query within a given topic, or on which learning materials are considered more appropriate to fulfill the students requests.

In such situations, trusting the end service provider, for instance with regard to adherence to the deliverys deadline, or with regard to compliance with the advertised quality of the learning material or the privacy constraints of the students personal information, may depend on the experience of other entities with the prospective service provider.

Based on that, a possible extension of the existing centralized SOA approaches to service discovery and selection is to investigate evaluation mechanisms that can report on the quality of the interactions. Additionally, this extension should consider the community of peers-clients that can share their experiences obtained through previous interactions with service providers - as the source for both service discovery and service selection.

3 State of the Art

As discussed in the previous sections, the distributed nature of SOA applications and the high-level description of its services offer, on the one hand, flexibility in business processes, but on the other hand, expose the involved parties to several potential risks and points of attack.

While trust management aspects are typically not considered in actual SOA implementations, several variants of SOA attempt to provide some extensions for privacy issues. Some of these variants are realized in the model-driven and pattern-oriented SOA approaches, which have attempted to solve these issues by introducing the privacy in the form of an orchestration layer. This latter defines contexts related with the privacy constraints for refining the access control to users sensitive data [8].

However, the implementations of these SOA models are often bound tightly to the low-level security mechanisms such as the Public Key Infrastructure (PKI) systems, as it is the case in the PRIME EU project [6]. This fact represents a major limitation for the fulfillment of higher-level and non-functional requirements such as the requirements on the assessment of trust [8][9].

Due to this fact, we argue that the context layer of SOA applications need to be extended in order to consider these factors, so that the requirements for modeling, representing and assessing trust can be taken into consideration. In the following section more details on this potential extension shall be discussed.

4   Solution

In order to demonstrate the applicability of our solution more concretely, we base the above-discussed extension on the work done in [1] [2] and [10], which aimed at improving the practices of designing and using the CURE system as a collaborative web-based learning application.

Within this approach, different layers have been identified and derived from the SOA life-cycle in order to enable an abstract level, called *conceptual level*, to be defined on the top of the architectural as well as the executional levels as shown in Figure 2. The idea behind the conceptual level is to contrast the functional requirements in the classical SOA implementations with additional non-functional requirements, which are intended to specify criteria that can be used to judge the operation of a system, rather than specific behaviors or functions. Making use of this feature, non-specific trust and privacy extensions can be realized within the existing CURE implementation.

The proposed approach for extending collaborative SOA applications with a trust assessment model can be broken down into the following tasks:

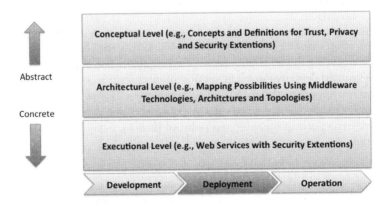

Fig. 2. Research Cluster for Collaborative SOA Applications

4.1   Modeling Trust

This task identifies the aspects pertaining to the trust assessment procedure in order to establish unified notations and schemes for representing the entities in the collaborative environment (for example, identifiers for the service providers as interaction partners in the distributed eLearning scenario), the trust-related attributes and metrics, such as the trust level, the scale for encoding the trust levels in homogenous manner (for example 1 for absolute trust and 0 for absolute distrust), the context of the interactions, which may refer to situational details characterizing the nature of the trust relationship between entities, as well as the environment surrounding them. In this study we consider trust between the end user and the service provider to be established for a certain *trust context*, for example trusting the service provider with regard to delivery deadlines may be different from trusting the quality of the learning material it shares in the collaborative environment.

This modeling, which shall be performed on the conceptual level, may include any other related aspects that can be needed in the trust quantification process.

4.2   Assessment of Trust

On the same level, different types of algorithms for assessing trust can be settled on the basis of the formal representation of trust. As investigated in [5], we base the trust assessment algorithms on two different logical computation methods:

– *Trust from past experiences* is an objective quantification method of trust on the basis of automatic evaluation of previous interactions, i.e. verification of the compliance of the interaction's result with the agreements [4]. The agreements in most of the interorganizational scenarios can be based on the Quality of Service (QoS) parameters as well as performance indicators and constraints on the functional level as well as on the financial levels. These paramters prove to be helpful for an organization to assess if the collaboration is running according to expectations. In this regard, defining suitable QoS parameters helps deciding what exactly is considered as trustful action execution.

  Therefore, in the context of the previous scenario, it is necessary for every organization member (service provider) to identify its performance indicators before engaging in the collaborative environment. For this issue, we propose a fine-grained description of the quality of interactions, such as describing the shared learning material with quality parameters. Based on that, we conclude that the trust level for a given quality parameter of a given interaction can be expressed as percentage, at given point of time t_0, according to the following equation:

$$T_\phi(t_0) = 100\% - \frac{\sum failedInteraction_\phi(t_0)}{\sum interaction_\phi(t_0)} \tag{1}$$

ϕ represents in the general case the association between the collaboration interactions (actions respectively resource) with the quality paramters referring thus to a distinct trust context.

For example, we associate the action *delivery* to a quality paramter *average time*, which is set to a certain period limit. A failed interaction for this context represents, thus, the case when the delivery exceeds the agreed upon limit.

Since we consider principally the failed requests from the total amount of interactions or verficiations, we have to subtract the resulting percentage from 100% in order to get the desired trust values in the *trust scale* of $[0, 1]$, where 0 represents complete distrust and 1 represents complete trust as stated in the previous item for modeling trust.

- *Trust by reputation* is a subjective quantification method for reasoning about trust by reputation, in a form of exchanged ratings. These ratings enable the creation of a feedback loop by reporting on actions of other parties [3]. However, one important issue that one should not neglect is the fact that the ratings, on the one hand, must be assigned according to the same trust scale of $[0, 1]$, and on the other hand, they must correspond to the quality paramters as discussed in order to reduce the effect of potential arbitrariness of individual partners ratings.

4.3   Aggregation of Trust

The different trust levels, which can result from the different computation methods (in this paper, trust from past experiences and trust by reputation), might be unequal or even contradictory, therefore, this step handles the verification of the different results, aggregates them and generates the final trust level of the interaction partner [4].

1: **if** $((\exists T_\phi^{past})$ and $(\nexists T_\phi^{reputation}))$ **then**
2:      $T_\phi^{final} = T_\phi^{past}$
3: **end if**
4: **if** $((\nexists T_\phi^{past})$ and $(\exists T_\phi^{reputation}))$ **then**
5:      $T_\phi^{final} = T_\phi^{reputation}$
6: **end if**

In this context, an aggregation algorithm for analyzing and aggregating the different trust levels has been investigated in [5]. The simplest form of this algorithm is the situation when just one single trust value is available for the given trust context. As can be seen in the listing example, this value shall be considered as the final trust level, in such a way that no aggregation is needed.

In the opposite case, where the trust values exists from more than one trust dimension, an aggregation rule is needed. The algorithm in this case attempts to match the given values in a single final value. While the computation of the trust level from past experience is performed automatically (after each interaction) by means of the monitoring tools, the trust level by reputation can be assessed only if at least one interaction partner leaves a rating level at the end of the

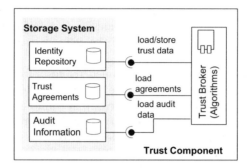

Fig. 3. The trust Component

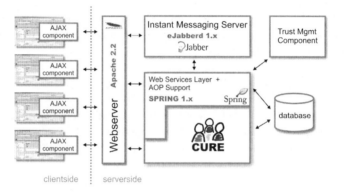

Fig. 4. Integration of the trust component within the CURE system

interaction. Due to this fact, the aggregation function sets up trust value from past experiences as the starting value and increments it or decrements with trust value by reputation according to the update function, which is detailed in [5].

4.4   Architectural Components

The realization of the sketched trust model is envisaged within the architectural level through a unified trust component. This component has for main task the implementation of the mentioned algorithms and methodologies as a set of distinct packages within a trust broker, which in turn is tightly coupled with an additional storage component, that manages the storage of the trust information (trust level), the inter-organizational agreements as well as the audit information for rating the interactions as input information for the quantification method of assessing trust from past experiences (see Figure 3).

Figure 4 shows an alternative for the integration of the trust component within the CURE system through a direct connection with the external messaging service (eJabberd), which allows synchronous Instant Messaging as well as Presence Awareness to take place.

Policy and Access Control

This task, which is realized in the executional level, aims at extending the existing authorization policies and access control decisions with the trust level that might be required for performing a given action or for acquiring a given right. This will be achieved in the form of an Access Decision Engine (ADE) [5]. In this aim, integrating trust management in the access control approach aims at including additional conditions along with the access control model; so that a requestor can decide about the service provider by checking its advertised quality parameters as well as its related trustworthiness to these parameters represented in the so-called trust levels.

5 Conclusions and Future Work

In this paper, we presented a method for extending the static access control models of SOA-based applications with a trust model with regard to service usage and resource consuming in collaborative eLearning environments.

This extension is based on appraising, updating, and aggregating the trust level of the service provider by its reputation that can be assigned by the end users as well as from its past interactions, which can be dynamically compared with the agreed upon agreements in order to enable a notion of history to be taken into account, and thus its trustworthiness to be assessed.

Additionally, in this study, the monitoring of the interactions not only affects the currently effective trust agreements, but also triggers a counter-measure automatically if some constraints are violated repeatedly. The selection of suitable QoS parameters, however, depends, among other things, on the possibilities to actually measure the indicators.

Currently, we investigated the relevant algorithms for this task on the conceptual level. The implementation of the trust component within the CURE system is still a work in progress.

References

1. Bourimi, M.: Collaborative design and tailoring of web based learning environments in CURE. In: Dimitriadis, Y.A., Zigurs, I., Gómez-Sánchez, E. (eds.) CRIWG 2006. LNCS, vol. 4154, pp. 421–436. Springer, Heidelberg (2006)
2. Bourimi, M., Lukosch, S., Khnel, F.: Leveraging visual tailoring and synchronous awareness in web-based collaborative systems. In: Haake, J.M., Ochoa, S.F., Cechich, A. (eds.) CRIWG 2007. LNCS, vol. 4715, pp. 40–55. Springer, Heidelberg (2007)
3. Boursas, L., Danciu, V.: Dynamic inter-organizational cooperation setup in circle-of-trust environments. In: Proceedings of the 20th IEEE Network Operations and Management Symposium NOMS 2008, Salvador, Brazil (2008)
4. Boursas, L., Hommel, W.: Multidimensional dynamic trust management for federated services. In: Proceedings of the IEEE/IFIP International Symposium on Trusted Computing and Communications (TrustCom 2009), Vancouver, Canada (August 2009)

5. Boursas, L.: Trust-Based Access Control in Federated Environments. PhD thesis, Technische Universität München, Munich, Germany, Technische Universität München, Munich, Germany (March 2009)
6. Camenisch, J., Crane, S., Fischer-Hübner, S., Leenes, R., Pearson, S., Pettersson, J.S., Sommer, D., Andersson, C.: Trust in prime. In: Proceedings of the Fifth IEEE International Symposium on Signal Processing and Information Technology, December 2005, pp. 552–559 (2005)
7. Haake, J.M., Schümmer, T., Haake, A., Bourimi, M., Landgraf, B.: Supporting flexible collaborative distance learning in the cure platform. In: Hawaii International Conference on System Sciences, vol. 1, p. 10003a. IEEE Computer Society Press, Los Alamitos (2004)
8. Hafner, M., Breu, R.: Security Engineering for Service-oriented Architectures. Springer, Heidelberg (October 2008)
9. Klarl, H.: Modellgetriebene, mustergestützte Sicherheit in serviceorientierten Architekturen. Informatik Spektrum 30(3), 175–177 (2007)
10. Lukosch, S., Bourimi, M.: Towards an enhanced adaptability and usability of web-based collaborative systems. International Journal of Cooperative Information Systems, Special Issue on Design and Implementation of Groupware, 467–494 (2008)

Author Index

Printing: Mercedes-Druck, Berlin
Binding: Stein+Lehmann, Berlin